a-b-c Shorthand

Stenoscript®

MANUEL C. AVANCENA

Revisions by Glenn J. Baldwin

Manufactured in the United States of America

STENOSCRIPT—registered trade mark
U.S. Patent Office

First Edition	- 1950
Revised	- 1951
Second Edition	- 1951
Revised	- 1956
Revised	- 1958
Revised	- 1959
Third Edition	- 1961
Revised	- 1961
Revised	- 1962
Revised	- 1963
Revised	- 1964
Revised	- 1965
Revised	- 1967

Published by
STENOSCRIPT ABC SHORTHAND, INC.
1570 MAPLE AVENUE
EVANSTON, ILLINOIS 60204

TABLE OF CONTENTS

DEDICATION

This edition of STENOSCRIPT ABC SHORTHAND is dedicated to the thousands of teachers who, by presenting this subject so effectively, have proven its worth and made it the fastest growing shorthand in the world — and — to the millions of students who, in pursuing this "almost miraculous" shorthand system, will be able to secure easier and better positions and provide a better way of life for themselves and their families.

These are a few of the teachers who have made major contributions in the improvement and refinement of STENOSCRIPT ABC SHORTHAND.

BIANCO, John R.   LONGLEY, Evalyn

CASARY, Carl   MOOSHAGIAN, Janet

CONNER, C. V.   NAGURSKI, Stephanie

DUNN, Margaret   SERGENT, V. R.

FITZPATRICK, Valarie   STOKES, Paul

HARDEN, Jacquelin   STRLE, Beatrice

OLIVER, Jeanne

INTRODUCTION

A. THE IDEA BEHIND THE THEORY

The purpose of this course is to enable you to master shorthand in the shortest time, at the least expense and at speeds necessary for government stenographers, secretaries, college students and those who must attend business conferences and meetings without the luxury of a secretary.

Since the first shorthand book using letters of the alphabet instead of symbols was printed, about fifty books on the same idea have been published. These books have improved on the original idea but are not necessarily derived from it; i.e., many persons have naturally found a necessity for a brief form of writing and have then attempted to systematize their ideas.

The writers of the later books either missed their mark because of the lack of statistical information, failed in their presentation of the method in text form, or failed to grasp the value of current books for dictation purposes.

It is generally conceded that all successful shorthand systems are based upon phonetic spelling. The success of a shorthand system is also dependent upon how much reduction in writing can be made from longhand.

STENOSCRIPT ABC SHORTHAND is a phonetic system of shorthand. By learning the 43 easy rules of STENOSCRIPT ABC SHORTHAND you will reduce the amount of your longhand writing by approximately 2/3. Simple arithmetic shows that if you reduce your writing by 2/3 — you can write three times as much in the same period of time. Since most people can write longhand at 35 to 40 words a minute — this means that by learning STENOSCRIPT ABC SHORTHAND you should be able to write 100-120 words a minute.

In STENOSCRIPT ABC SHORTHAND you can attain a speed of 80 words a minute with comparatively little effort, while a speed of 100 words a minute is attainable by earnest study. Higher speeds can be reached over the same period depending upon the individual. Furthermore, the notes can be transcribed a month or even a year later because only the alphabet and familiar punctuation marks are used.

With statistical information made available through research by such men as Leonard P. Ayres and Edward L. Thorndike it is known that the greatest part of all writing is made up of only a few words. This fact has made the alphabetical shorthand system a science, a science which has correlated several characteristics of the English language and has set forth a logical system of writing it as fast as it is normally dictated.

The STENOSCRIPT ABC SHORTHAND dictionary includes the one thousand most common words used in the English language. Statistics show that fifty of these words make up one-half of all written words.

Beyond these thousand words the accuracy of frequency of occurrence is difficult to determine without error because words used vary according to the subject or business in which they are used. Nevertheless, our dictionary contains over 5,000 words which were compiled in order of frequency of occurrence along with other business and technical words of common usage.

Three hundred words of the thousand words constitute three-fourths of all written words and the thousand most common words make up about nine-tenths of all written words.

Are you surprised to know that **the, of, I, to, in, a, that, you** and **for** comprise one-fourth of all written words?

One of the characteristics of the English language, as pointed out in the ''Funk and Wagnalls Standard Dictionary'', is that unstressed vowels are more or less ''obscured'' in the utterance. This means that consonants or hard-sounding letters cause most of the verbal work. This fact is also important in the underlying theory of this system. Usually, all that is written of a word are its letters representing the dominant sounds which are usually consonants; i.e., all letters except **a, e, i, o** and **u,** which are vowels.

Another important part of this system is found in the use of the prefix and the suffix. Statistics show that the prefix **un** precedes six thousand words in a list of twenty thousand most used words and that **er, or, ty, ible, ive** and **ance** follow nine thousand words on this list.

At this point you may find a brief explanation on words and their make-up helpful since some understanding is essential to the study of any shorthand system.

A primitive or base word is one which is not derived from any other word in the language, as **stand, man** and **right.**

A derivative or compound word is one which is derived from another word, as **understand, manly** and **rightfully.**

Compound words are formed from base words by means of particles. These particles may be placed before or after base words.

Particles placed before base words are called prefixes, as **un** in **unrest** and **under** in **understand.**

Particles placed after base words are called suffixes, as **ing** in **writing** and **tion** in **education.**

B. THE VOWEL AND THE DOMINANT SOUND

The first and fundamental rule in this system is that all vowels are omitted from a word (except as noted below). As stated in Part A, the vowel is obscured in the utterance and the consonants do the verbal work. Because of this, the vowels perform a special function in this system as you shall see in the **accentuated vowel** rule.

Exceptions to omitting vowels:

(1) Whenever they are sounded at the beginning or end of words (Lesson I, Rule 3).

(2) When the **accentuated vowel** rule is used (Lesson IV, Rule 1).

C. HOW TO STUDY STENOSCRIPT ABC SHORTHAND

The study of STENOSCRIPT ABC SHORTHAND is divided into two separate phases. The first is the learning of the theory which is presented in only seven lessons. The second is putting the theory into practice and attaining a speed in STENOSCRIPT ABC SHORTHAND that will enable you to secure and hold a position as an efficient secretary or a stenographer. This second phase of the course is accomplished by dictation and using the theory you have learned in the first seven lessons. You will actually start taking dictation at approximately 60 words a minute and your speed will be increased daily so that by the end of the course you will have reached a speed in STENOSCRIPT ABC SHORTHAND that would have taken you from 3 to 10 times as long if you had studied any other shorthand system.

According to shorthand experts, only one-tenth of one per cent of those who study shorthand are able to attain speeds necessary for verbatim court reporting and similar jobs that require extremely high speeds.

If you are interested in that type of work, a machine method is suggested. But, if you want to be a secretary or want to take notes and letters at ordinary dictation speeds, you are learning the best system because you learn it in the shortest time with the least effort.

Although this shorthand course is relatively easy, you should consider it intense.

You must study every day. Each weekend you must take dictation and study both Saturday and Sunday.

It should not be necessary to spend more than an hour studying each day.

The reward to you for consistency in study is well worth the time and effort. You acquire the knowledge in a short time that your friends take years to learn. As a result you are eligible for whatever increases in pay and promotion that may be available to you as a stenographer.

The entire theory is covered in seven lessons and the remainder of the course is devoted to building your speed and increasing your accuracy in putting longhand into shorthand.

YOU WILL LEARN TO TAKE DICTATION AND TRANSCRIBE IT BY RULES. EVERYTHING YOU DO MUST BE LOGICAL AND THERE MUST BE A REASON FOR DOING IT.

In all good shorthand systems sound plays a major part. You will learn that it plays an important part in this system. Briefly, you put into shorthand what you hear of a word by using letters of the alphabet and punctuation marks to represent those sounds.

You will learn that the thought of a sentence or paragraph also plays an important part in this system as an aid to transcribing what you have put into shorthand. This aid is known as the "context of the sentence." For instance, when a word cannot be transcribed by itself, the whole sentence taken together will suggest the correct word. Or, when two different words are written the same way in shorthand and it is difficult to transcribe the word standing alone, you will find that the context of the sentence or paragraph will aid you. When using the shorthand of the basic form of the word, the whole sentence taken together suggests the proper form of the word as it was intended by the dictator.

STENOSCRIPT ABC SHORTHAND theory is divided into five different categories. A brief explanation of each category follows:

I Dominant Sounds: The dominant sounds in words are the basis of all good shorthand systems. It is actually very simple and means that you write only the sounds that you hear in a word. (Usually this means omitting vowel sounds within words as they are usually silent.) Writing dominant sounds may also be referred to as phonetic spelling.

II High-Frequency Words: These are words in our language that are used more frequently than others. You probably will be surprised to know that approximately 50 words make up half of an ordinary conversation. These words are usually personal pronouns, articles, simple verbs or prepositions (**he, you; the,** *an; go, am; at, of).* Because these words are used so frequently, it is very important in a shorthand system that you write as little as possible for these words. In STENOSCRIPT ABC SHORTHAND each high-frequency word is reduced to one or two letters of the alphabet.

III High-Frequency Letter-Groups: In our language there are certain groups of letters which occur more frequently than others. An example would be *th.* You find this combination used in hundreds of words such as *this, that, those,* etc. In STENOSCRIPT ABC SHORTHAND each high-frequency letter-group is reduced to a letter of the alphabet or a punctuation mark.

IV Prefixes and Suffixes: Words of more than one syllable are usually divided into their component parts: prefix, root, suffix — as the case may be. The root is the primitive word; i.e., that part of the word not derived from another word in our language. Because prefixes and suffixes are so common in our language, in STENOSCRIPT ABC SHORTHAND write the fewest possible letters to represent them.

V Additional Aids: Additional aids are rules and devices to further reduce the amount of writing in STENOSCRIPT ABC SHORTHAND. These cover such things as expressions of time, measurements, days of the week, months of the year, etc.

You will study the elements of these five categories in the following seven theory lessons.

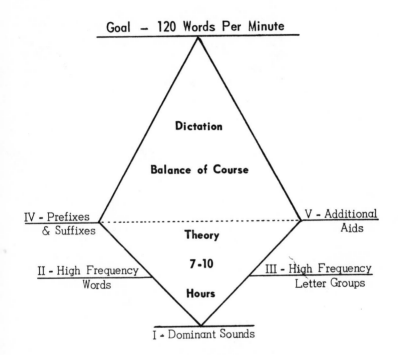

Goal — 120 Words Per Minute

Dictation

Balance of Course

IV - Prefixes & Suffixes

V - Additional Aids

Theory

7-10

II - High Frequency Words

III - High Frequency Letter Groups

Hours

I - Dominant Sounds

Begin — 35-40 Words Per Minute

(Average Longhand Speed)

NOTES

1. In writing shorthand your hand should always move in a forward direction; therefore, you never go back to cross a *t* or dot an *i* or *j*. To distinguish clearly between *t* and *l*, or *i* and *e*, be sure to close letters *t* and *i* and loop letters *l* and *e*. Always write these letters as follows: *t* _____; *l* _____; *i* _____; *e* _____; *j* _____.

2. The Dominant-Sound rule: The dominant-sound rule is simply that in STENOSCRIPT ABC SHORTHAND you write only the letters of the alphabet that represent the sounds you hear in a word; i.e., the phonetic spelling of the word. Always remember that the longhand spelling of a word is not important because STENOSCRIPT ABC SHORTHAND is always written based on the way a word sounds. Do not write vowel sounds (*a, e, i, o* and *u*) within a base word. Each letter represents its own sound as pronounced.

PRACTICE WORDS:

because		differ	_____	middle	_____
better		*does	_____	package	_____
bitten	_____	*doze	_____	pepper	_____
book	_____	fancy	_____	pocket	_____
bottom	_____	favor	_____	quit	_____
box	_____	give	_____	quiver	_____
cab	_____	good	_____	recall	_____
cage	_____	has	_____	recess	_____
car	_____	judge	_____	refer	_____
cater	_____	jug	_____	regency	_____
censor	_____	ledger	_____	rose	_____
cider	_____	letter	_____	sell	_____
cigar	_____	level	_____	settle	_____
cipher	_____	matter	_____	size	_____
civil	_____	maze	_____	some	_____
damage	_____	metal	_____	ticket	_____

*In STENOSCRIPT ABC SHORTHAND, as in longhand, you will on occasion write different words the same way. You will be able to determine the proper word and transcribe it correctly because of the context of the sentence in which the word is used. To illustrate, the word **well** written by itself fails to tell you if it is **how you feel,** an **exclamation** or a **hole in the ground** until you put the word into a sentence.

   3. Write vowel sounds (**a, e, i, o** and **u**) at the beginning or end of a base word. Do not write vowel sounds within a base word.

PRACTICE WORDS:

agency	*ajnc*	engine	_____	low	_____
above	_____	funny	_____	may	*ma*
argue	_____	high	_____	money	*mne*
defy	_____	honey	_____	offer	_____
easy	_____	icy	_____	office	_____
edge	_____	incur	_____	pay	*pa*
embezzle	_____	knew	_____	rely	_____
endeavor	_____	lay	_____	sunny	_____

   4. Whenever a word ends in a double consonant sound, write only the more predominant of the two sounds (usually the first of the two sounds).

PRACTICE WORDS:

adopt	*adp*	except	_____	left	_____
attempt	_____	exempt	_____	object	_____
detect	_____	expect	_____	soft	_____
eject	_____	fact	_____	task	_____

5. The small letter **c** represents the **ch** sound.

PRACTICE WORDS:

attach _____*alc*_____   reach _____

cheese _____   such _____*ac*_____

kitchen _____   teach _____*lc*_____

much _____*mc*_____   which _____*wc*_____

6. To add **d** or **ed** to any base word in STENOSCRIPT ABC SHORTHAND merely underline the last letter of the shorthand. This rule provides the past tense to regular verbs.

PRACTICE WORDS:

fix _____*fx*_____   fixed _____*fx*_____

cause _____   caused _____

chop _____*cp*_____   chopped _____*cp*_____

7. Singular and plural: Plural forms of nouns are not written in STENOSCRIPT ABC SHORTHAND. The context of a sentence will indicate whether they are singular or plural.

8. Use regular punctuation in STENOSCRIPT ABC SHORTHAND. Although the comma is used in STENOSCRIPT ABC SHORTHAND to represent a high-frequency letter-group (LESSON V), it is, when so used, attached to the preceding letter so it will not be confused with the comma used separately as punctuation.

9. Paragraphing: To indicate a new paragraph use two slant marks (//) and continue writing on the same line.

10. Standard abbreviations:

     a. For countries, states and cities use standard abbreviations.

     b. If any other standard abbreviation you are accustomed to using is shorter than the complete shorthand for the word, use the standard abbreviation, as **RR** for **railroad.**

11. High-frequency words are a very important part of a shorthand system. You should learn these words and the correct shorthand for them so that, as soon as you hear one of them, you immediately write the correct shorthand.

GROUP I (High-Frequency Words)

a		do		had	
an	a	dew		have	h
and	↲	due	d	having	
		did			
		done		I	I
be		doing			
been				if	
being				it	i
by	b	he	e		
bye		me		is	
buy					
but		for	f	can	
				come	
		go		came	k
see		goes		coming	
seen	c	gone	g		
seeing		going			

12

LESSON II

In Lesson I you have covered dominant sounds, the basis of STENOSCRIPT ABC SHORTHAND and some high-frequency words. In Lesson II you will study some high-frequency letter-groups and also several additional aids.

1. The dash (–) is used to represent the following: The high-frequency word **the** and the high-frequency letter-group sounds of **th, nd, nt, mand, mond, mend** and **ment**. When used to represent a high-frequency letter-group sound, the dash is always connected to the letter preceding or following it, so that the continuity of your writing is not broken. Your speed is not affected because it is unnecessary to lift your pencil or pen from the paper. The dash may be written at any length.

PRACTICE WORDS:

bath		find		rather	
beneath		gather		resident	
cement		gentle		sent	
death		handle		teeth	
*defiant		invent		tent	
demand		judgment		them	
either		kind		then	
event		leather		thick	
evident		lend		vend	
expand		oath		want	
extent		patent		window	
father		*payment		winter	

13

NOTE: When you have a word that is written with a double dash the two dashes are connected with a slight jog. For example the word **amendment** would be written _𝑎___.

*As stated in Rule 3, Lesson I, do not write a vowel sound within a base word. In derivatives, however, like **defiant** and **payment** where the base word ends in a vowel sound, write the base word and then add the suffix. In these two instances the word **defiant** is written _𝑑𝑓𝑒___ and the word **payment** is written _𝑝𝑎___.

2. The small letter **g** represents the **ng** sound.

PRACTICE WORDS:

among	_𝑎𝑚𝑔_	eating	_____	ringing	_____
backing	_____	hang	_____	single	_____
boxing	_____	long	_____	wrong	_____

3. The small letter **j** represents the **shun** sound.

PRACTICE WORDS:

action	_𝑎𝑘𝑗_	mention	_____
attention	_____	nation	_____
decision	_____	occasion	_____
education	_____	pension	_____

14

4. The small letter **z** represents the **sh** sound.

PRACTICE WORDS:

cash	*kz*	push	_____	shoe	_____
finish	_____	rush	_____	shop	_____
fish	_____	shall	_____	should	_____
issue	_____	shell	_____	wish	_____

5. The small letter **q** represents the **nk** sound.

PRACTICE WORDS:

bank	*bq*	rink	_____	think	_____
ink	_____	sink	_____	zinc	_____

6. Do not write an **l** or an **r** sound within a base word unless it is accentuated. Always write an **l** or an **r** sound at the beginning or end of a word.

PRACTICE WORDS:

along	*alq*	current	_____	former	_____
belong	_____	delay	_____	margin	_____
caress	_____	deliver	_____	perform	_____
carriage	_____	enrich	_____	perish .	_____
cellar	_____	firm	_____	person	_____
clever	_____	follow	_____	policy	_____
correct	_____	forbid	_____	pretend	_____
critic	_____	forget	_____	process	_____

(PRACTICE WORDS, Rule 6, Continued)

product	_____	purse	_____	singular	_____
program	_____	qualify	_____	traffic	_____
project	_____	quarrel	_____	travel	_____
promise	_____	regular	_____	truck	_____
protect	_____	service	_____	warrant	_____

7. GROUP II (High-Frequency Words):

will		or		saw	
well	l	so		us	s
all		on	o		
my		owe		at	
am	m			to	t
many		out	O	too	
him				two	
in		up	p		
no		are			
know		our			
neither	n	hour	r		
nor		her			
not					
none					

16

LESSON III

1. The slant (/) represents the high-frequency letter-group sounds of **rd, rt, rk** and **ward.**

PRACTICE WORDS:

accord	*ak/*	dark	_____	order	_____
afford	_____	department	_____	pardon	_____
alert	_____	deport	_____	regard	_____
*apartment	_____	effort	_____	report	_____
assert	_____	expert	_____	sort	_____
backward	_____	guard	_____	support	_____
board	_____	heard	_____	toward	_____
card	_____	mark	_____	word	_____
court	_____	*mortal	_____	work	_____

*Whenever you have words like **apartment** and **mortal** where a slant is used within a word, you continue writing at the top of the slant. You do not return to the line of writing to finish the word. The word **apartment** is written ___ *ap/* ___ and **mortal** is written ___ *ml* ___.

2. The small letter **y** represents the **oi** sound and the **ry** sound.

PRACTICE WORDS:

annoy	*any*	choice	_____	join	_____	voice	_____
appoint	_____	enjoy	_____	point	_____	battery	_____
boy	_____	foil	_____	toil	_____	carry	_____

17

(PRACTICE WORDS, Rule 2, Continued)

century _____ grocery _____ jury _____ sorry _____

delivery _____ hurry _____ misery _____ worry _____

3. The small letter *m* represents the sound of the prefix **mis.**

PRACTICE WORDS:

mishap   *mhp*   misjudge _____

mishandle _____   misprint   _____

4. The capital **N** represents the **ntr** sound.

PRACTICE WORDS:

enter   *n*   intermittent _____

enterprise _____   intermix   _____

interview   _____   intersect   _____

interject   _____   interval   _____

interlapse _____   interworking _____

5. The small letter *d* represents the **dis** and **des** sounds at the beginning of a word.

PRACTICE WORDS:

disagree   *dage*   discard   _____

disappoint _____   discuss   _____

disband   _____   disorder _____

18

6. GROUP III (High-Frequency Words):

you		we		why	y
your	u	were			
			w	as	
yours		who			
				was	
		whom			z
under	U			his	
		of		she	
over	V		v		
		very			

7. Salutation and complimentary close:

(These words are written using these abreviations only when used as part of the salutation or close.)

a. This group is commonly used in business letters:

Dear ___*d*___

Dear Sir ___*ds*___   Yours truly ___*ul*___

Dear Madam ___*dm*___   Very truly yours ___*vlu*___

Gentlemen ___*g*___   Yours very truly ___*uvl*___

b. This group is commonly used in informal letters:

Dear Mr. ___*dmr*___   Yours sincerely ___*us*___

Dear Miss ___*dme*___   Sincerely yours ___*su*___

Dear Mrs. ___*dms*___   Cordially yours ___*cu*___

Respectfully yours ___*ru*___   Respectfully ___*r*___

19

NOTES

LESSON IV

1. The **accentuated vowel** rule is a real advancement in the science of shorthand. It is one of the main reasons that you learn to write STENOSCRIPT ABC SHORTHAND proficiently after only a few hours of instruction. The **accentuated vowel** rule is one of the easiest rules in STENOSCRIPT ABC SHORTHAND to learn. The rule is this:

When the final single-consonant sound of a base word is preceded by a long or accentuated vowel sound, write the word through this long or accentuated vowel sound and drop the final consonant sound.

A good general rule for applying the accentuated vowel rule is: When you hear a **long** vowel sound near the end of a base word, write the word through this **long** vowel sound and stop writing. In other words, write through the accentuated vowel sound.

NOTE: The **accentuated vowel** rule will be used on some words in which the first vowel sound is not a true long vowel. These are words ending in the **air-are** and **ere-ear** sounds. For example the word **hear** is written _*he*_ and the word **pair** is written _*pa*_ .

PRACTICE WORDS:

alone	*alo*	deed	_____	fire	_____	like	_____
appeal	_____	delete	_____	here	_____	load	_____
bribe	_____	duke	_____	hike	_____	loaf	_____
broke	_____	expire	_____	home	_____	loan	_____
care	_____	face	_____	hope	_____	loose	_____
cheap	_____	fake	_____	knife	_____	made	_____
chief	_____	fame	_____	lane	_____	mail	_____
clean	_____	feel	_____	late	_____	more	_____
comb	_____	file	_____	leaf	_____	near	_____
creak	_____	fine	_____	life	_____	neat	_____

21

(PRACTICE WORDS, Rule 1, Continued)

nice _____	race _____	safe _____	suit _____
niece _____	rate _____	sale _____	sure _____
night _____	ream _____	scheme _____	take _____
note _____	resume _____	shade _____	tape _____
phone _____	ride _____	shame _____	time _____
piece _____	robe _____	shape _____	trade _____
plane _____	role _____	share _____	trial _____
pole _____	rope _____	side _____	tune _____
price _____	rude _____	smoke _____	type _____
pursuit _____	rule _____	soon _____	vote _____

NOTE: There are 3 exceptions to the accentuated vowel rule. When a **long** vowel sound is followed by a **j, v** or **z** sound, these letters will be written instead of the **long** vowel sound because their sound is more predominant than that of the long vowel. Examples: – **maze** _mz_ ; **believe** _blv_ ; **cage** _kj_ .

2. The capital letter **S** represents the **st** sound.

PRACTICE WORDS:

accost	_akS_	custom	_____	ghost	_____
adjustment	_____	digest	_____	highest	_____
assist	_____	distrust	_____	history	_____
best	_____	enlistment	_____	honest	_____
cost	_____	fast	_____	just	_____

22

(PRACTICE WORDS, Rule 2, Continued)

least	_____	rest	_____	stern	_____
minister	_____	roast	_____	stock	_____
most	_____	sister	_____	stone	_____
nest	_____	steam	_____	story	_____
pastor	_____	steel	_____	strict	_____
protest	_____	stem	_____	toast	_____
resist	_____	step	_____	worst	_____

3. GROUP IV (High-Frequency Words)

after	af	from	fm	those	—oz
again	ag	off	of	there	—r
against		often		their	
begin		any	ne	this	—s
began	bg	never	nv		
begun				that	—t
beginning		upon	pn		
even		which	wc	these	—z
ever	ev			with	w—
every		they	—a	whose	wz

23

NOTES

LESSON V

1. The comma (,) is used to represent the *ity* sound. It also represents the *nce* sound. When so used it is always attached to the preceding letter.

PRACTICE WORDS:

abundance	*ab*	fence		patience	
appearance		finality		pity	
annoyance		finance		quality	
appliance		glance		quantity	
calamity		gravity		reliance	
capacity		gritty		sense	
clearance		identity		sentence	
city		locality		silence	
defiance		majority		suspense	
dominance		maternity		utility	
dunce		minority		vicinity	
facility		once		witty	

2. The capital letter **B** represents the **ble** sound.

PRACTICE WORDS:

bible	*bB*	fashionable		suitable	
cable		liable		table	
capable		possible		touchable	
double		stable		workable	

25

3. The small letter **k** represents the sounds of **com** and **con** at the beginning of a word.

PRACTICE WORDS:

comfort	*kf*	condemn	_____
compact	_____	condense	_____
compass	_____	confident	_____
compel	_____	consent	_____

4. The capital letter **K** represents the sounds **contr** and **counter.**

PRACTICE WORDS:

| contradict | *Kdk* | counteract | _____ |
| controversy | _____ | counterfeit | _____ |

5. The small letter **x** represents the sounds **eus, shul** and **shus.**

PRACTICE WORDS:

devious	*dux*	social	_____
gracious	_____	spacious	_____
official	_____	special	_____
partial	_____	various	_____

6. Brief Forms: In STENOSCRIPT ABC SHORTHAND there are 24 **brief forms** to be memorized. Each brief form applies to **any** form of the word it represents. _____*ak*_____ would represent not only **acknowledge** but also **acknowledgment** and **acknowledging**. Note that these brief forms do not necessarily conform to the rules of STENOSCRIPT ABC SHORTHAND. The list follows:

acknowledge	*ak*	individual	*ndv*
accompany	*ac*	information	*nfo*
accomplish	*ac*	manufacture	*mf*
administrate	*adm*	merchandise	*mds*
appreciate	*ap*	opportunity	*op*
approximate	*apx*	organize	*og*
association	*asn*	particular	*prl*
business	*bz*	represent	*rp*
company	*co*	responsible	*rsp*
corporation	*crp*	satisfy	*sl*
government	*gvl*	situation	*sil*
immediate	*imd*	specification	*spc*

27

NOTES

LESSON VI

1. The small letter **s** represents the **sub** sound.

PRACTICE WORDS:

subject	_sjk_	submit	_____
sublet	_____	subside	_____
sublime	_____	substance	_____
submerge	_____	substitute	_____

2. The small letter **v** represents the sound of the suffix **tive.**

PRACTICE WORDS:

attentive	_alnv_	detective	_____	relative	_____
descriptive	_____	protective	_____	selective	_____

3. The small letter **l** represents the **lee** sound at the end of a word.

PRACTICE WORDS:

badly	_bdl_	merely	_____	annually	_anll_
easily	_____	rapidly	_____	finally	_____
family	_____	sadly	_____	totally	_____

4. The small letter **a** represents the sound of the syllable **ad** at the beginning of a word.

PRACTICE WORDS:

adequate	_aql_	admire	_____	advantage	_____
adhere	_____	admit	_____	advise	_____

29

5. The capital letter **F** represents the sound of **ful** and **fully.**

PRACTICE WORDS:

fulfillment	_7ffl_	thankful	_____
fully	_____	watchful	_____
lawful	_____	wonderfully	_____

NOTE: One of the easiest ways to write a capital letter **F** is to make a figure seven and cross it. This lends itself to the easy writing of STENOSCRIPT ABC SHORTHAND and is also quite distinguishable as a capital letter **F** when transcribing.

6. The capital letter **C** represents the **circ** and **circum** sounds.

PRACTICE WORDS:

circle	_Cl_	circumflex	_____
circuit	_____	circumspect	_____
circular	_____	circumvent	_____

LESSON VII

1. The small letter **u** represents the sound of the prefix **un.**

PRACTICE WORDS:

unbend *ub*   unhappy _____

uncut _____   unheard _____

uneasy _____   unpaid _____

unfair _____   unsafe _____

2. The capital letter **T** represents the sound of **trans** at the beginning of a word.

PRACTICE WORDS:

transact *Tak*   transit _____ transplant _____

transfer _____ transmit _____ transparent _____

transform _____ transmission _____ transport _____

3. The small letter **w** represents the **ow** sound.

PRACTICE WORDS:

house *hws*   mouse _____

allow _____   doubt _____

loud _____   tower _____

now _____   vowel _____

NOTE: Do not use the small letter **w** before the **nt** or **nd.** For example
account is written *ak* ; **around** is written *ar*
found is written *f* .

31

4. Days and Months: Days of the week and months of the year are put into shorthand by capitalizing the first letter of the word plus the next consonant. The exception is **January** which is written with the first letter capitalized and the first vowel, **Ja,** to distinguish it from **June.**

Sunday		January		July	
Monday		February		August	
Tuesday		March		September	
Wednesday		April		October	
Thursday		May		November	
Friday		June		December	
Saturday					

The words **day, week, month** and **year** are represented by the first letter of the word capitalized.

day   month

week   year

5. Time: _____ is **a.m.** and _____ is **p.m.** Therefore, any numeral with a small _____ or _____ following it is a symbol of time. For instance, **10:00 p.m.** is written _____.

32

SUMMARY OF STENOSCRIPT ABC SHORTHAND RULES

1. Do not cross *t*; do not dot *i* or *j*.

2. Always write the sounds you hear (**phonetic spelling**).

3. Write vowels (**a, e, i, o** and **u**) only if sounded at the beginning or end of a base word.

4. Whenever a word ends in a double consonant sound write only the most predominant of the two sounds.

5. The small letter **c** represents the **ch** sound.

6. To add **d** or **ed** for past tense underline the last letter of the shorthand.

7. Write nouns singular.

8. Use regular punctuation.

9. To indicate a new paragraph use two slant marks(//).

10. Use standard abbreviations.

11. High-frequency words are the most used words in our language and must be memorized.

12. The dash (—) is used to represent the following: the word **the** and the high-frequency letter-group sounds **th, nd, nt, mand, mond, mend** and **ment**.

13. The small letter **g** represents the **ng** sound.

14. The small letter **j** represents the **shun** sound.

15. The small letter **z** represents the **sh** sound.

16. The small letter **q** represents the **nk** sound.

17. Do not write an **l** or an **r** within a base word unless it is accentuated.

18. The slant (/) represents the high-frequency letter-group sounds **rd, rt, rk** and **ward**.

19. The small letter **y** represents the **oi** sound and the **ry** sound.

20. The small letter **m** represents the prefix sound of **mis**.

21. The capital letter **N** represents the **ntr** sound.

22. The small letter **d** represents the sounds of **dis** and **des**.

23. There are special forms for the salutation and complimentary close.

24. When the final consonant sound of a base word is preceded by a long vowel sound, write only the long vowel sound.

25. The capital letter **S** represents the **st** sound.

26. The comma (**,**) is used to represent the **ity** and **nce** sounds.

27. The capital letter **B** represents the **ble** sound.

28. The small letter **k** represents **com** and **con** sounds.

29. The capital letter **K** represents the sounds **contr** and **counter.**

30. The small letter **x** represents the sounds **eus, shul** and **shus.**

31. There are 24 **brief forms** to be memorized.

32. The small letter **s** represents the **sub** sound.

33. The small letter **v** represents the suffix sound of **tive.**

34. The small letter **l** represents the **lee** sound at the end of a word.

35. The small letter **a** represents the sound **ad** at the beginning of a word.

36. The capital letter **F** represents the sounds of **ful** and **fully.**

37. The capital letter **C** represents the sounds of **circ** and **circum.**

38. The small letter **u** represents the prefix sound of **un.**

39. The capital letter **T** represents the **trans** sound at the beginning of a word.

40. The small letter **w** represents the **ow** sound.

41. The days and months are put into shorthand by using the first letter of the word capitalized and the first consonant after the letter. The exception is **January** which is **Ja.**

42. The words **day, week, month** and **year** are represented by the first letter of each word capitalized.

43. The small letter **a** represents **a.m.** The small letter **p** represents **p.m.**

HOMEWORK SECTION

The material in this section is correlated with the text material, lesson for lesson. Thus, lesson I of this section will use only words employing rules in lesson I and letters in lesson IV will use only words using rules in lesson IV and previous lessons, etc.

Please note that all dictation material is marked off in 20-word groups to make it easy to dictate at timed speeds (see page 72).

NOTES

HOMEWORK

LESSON I

(/ indicates 20-word groups for dictating.)

1. I can use a pencil. He can buy me a pencil. I can use a pen. If he goes, see / if he can get me a pen. See if he can buy me some paper when he gets me a pen. If he gets me a pencil, a pen and some paper, I can pay for it. (57)

_____

_____

_____

_____

2. He has a dog. It is a big dog. If it is a good dog, he can buy it some / chops. If it is a bad dog, he can sell it. If I see a good dog, I pet it. / If I see a bad dog, I run. (48)

_____

_____

_____

3. He can teach me. He is a good teacher. He teaches me a new way. It is an easy way. / It is a quick way. I can get it much better when he teaches me a quick way. I can / get a bigger pay check because I do what he teaches me. (52)

_____

_____

_____

_____

4. Transcribe the following:

I h a kr. I kl i a gd kr wn i rn. i
hz a gd mtr. i i g bd I k h i fx. i e b
i e k pa e f i. i I c a btr kr I k b i.
I h sm mne & I k pa f i.

HOMEWORK

LESSON II

1. He told me to go for him. He said that he would pay me for it. If I knew he / would pay me, I would go. Some people say he does not pay any bills. (35)

_____

_____

_____

2. This is a good way to learn something new. It is so easy to do. If they had told me, / I would have done it before. If he thinks I am good, I may try to win. That would be / fun. Help me do it the way he says it is done so I will be chosen for a prize. (60)

_____

_____

_____

_____

3. He will get an education if he watches what they are doing. I would go with him if I could. / It would be an excellent way for me to see what is being done. I wish they would tell me / what they are doing so that I would not have to go to see if it is being done. I / think it is being handled well because the man that runs the office for me is a good office manager. (80)

_____

_____

_____

_____

_____

4. The man has a good job. He teaches in the new building they opened in the winter. He does the / job well because he is a good teacher. He does not let the children run the class. He does / not abuse them, but he is firm and they respect him. The children get a good education. He is respected / by the children and their mothers and fathers. For this reason, the children he teaches will get a good education. (80)

_____

_____

_____

_____

_____

_____

_____

5. Transcribe the following:

(shorthand)

_____

_____

_____

HOMEWORK

LESSON III

1. Dear Sir: Please send me back the equipment you borrowed from me. I want to use it on a new / job. You have had it longer than you expected. When you send it back, send me a check. Sincerely, (40)

_____

_____

_____

2. Dear Madam: I want you to use the sample I am sending you. You will find it will work better / than the kind you are using. Carry it with you when you go shopping. You will wonder if you can / do without it. Yours truly, (45)

_____

_____

_____

_____

3. Transcribe the following:

4. When learning a course such as this, it is very important that you come to class for each lesson. This / way you will learn a little each session and it will be very easy. You will have to put in / some extra work other than that which you do in class if you want to be ahead of the others. / Try to get plenty of extra dictation so that your teacher will be pleased with your progress. You will then / be in a position to demand a bigger pay check. (90)

5. Dear Sir: We are told you go hunting, and we want you to know why you should buy our new / gun. It has been used by experts who tell us it is a good gun. In fact, they say it / is a better gun than any they have used, and that they can hit a target from far away. They / say it is easy to insert shells in the chamber and that it is not too heavy. We want you / to try this new gun. Go to any gun shop and ask to try this gun without charge. Yours truly (100)

_____

_____

_____

_____

_____

_____

_____

6. Education pays big dividends. By learning shorthand, for example, you can qualify for a much better position. You will have / bigger pay checks and an easier job. It will also be easier for you to get a job if you / are not working. You can look in the paper and always find jobs that demand shorthand at better than average / pay. Learn your shorthand well, and you will not be without a good job. Shorthand is the shortcut to success. (80)

_____

_____

_____

_____

_____

_____

_____

NOTES

HOMEWORK

LESSON IV

1. Dear Sir: I would like to tell you that I think the cheese you sell is the best I have / eaten. The taste is different and most pleasing. Please send 3 dozen packages of this cheese to me. Send the / bill to my office. Sincerely, (45)

_____

_____

_____

_____

2. Gentlemen: The question you asked is rather hard to answer. We have done very little work along these lines. We / would suggest that you discuss this matter with a person who is more qualified to help you. Very truly yours, (45)

_____

_____

_____

_____

3. Travel is something we all like. Some of us prefer to travel by car. Others like to go by / bus and train while others feel that the speed of air travel is most important. We are sure to learn / many things regardless of which way we choose. When we travel by car, we can stop to rest often. / We can also stop at interesting places along the way. When we travel by train or bus, we have more / time to relax as well as the occasion to make friends. Travel by air is faster and a real time / and money item for those who must travel a lot. You should choose the way best suited to your needs. (120)

_____

_____

_____

_____

_____

_____

_____

_____

4. Dear Sir: We would like to hear from you soon. As you know, your bill is past due. We have / not had a payment from you for a long time. When we extend credit, we do it as a friend. / We want to remain a friend, but it is not easy if you do not make your payments as agreed. / If there is anything wrong with the goods you got from us, let us know and we will correct it. / If you do not have the money to make the payment at this time, just let us know when you / will make the payment and we will understand. If you can pay part of the bill, it would help our / friendship a lot. Please stop in or write and tell us when we can expect your next payment. Yours truly, (140)

_____

_____

_____

_____

_____

_____

_____

_____

_____

5. Dear Sir: Thank you for your recent order for a set of dishes. The set that you ordered is our / biggest seller. Your wife will be happy to have such a nice set of dishes. She will enjoy serving dinner / on them. You will both be happy to serve dinner to your friends on them. Should you ever break any / of the pieces, you can always be sure that we have this pattern in stock. Thank you very much for / buying these dishes from us. If you have any friends that need new dishes, please tell them that you are / happy with the dishes you got from us. We will not sell them the same pattern you have. Yours truly, (120)

_____

_____

_____

_____

_____

_____

_____

_____

_____

6. Transcribe the following:

[handwritten shorthand exercise]

HOMEWORK — LESSON IV

NOTES

HOMEWORK

LESSON V

1. Dear Sir: Since you last came to our store, we have been able to find some of the merchandise you / want. We can get it for you immediately and, like everything we sell, we promise you will be satisfied. If / you need more information, call me. Very truly yours, (50)

_____ _____

_____

_____

_____

_____

2. Dear Sir: We would like to have you represent us in your city. It is a real opportunity for you. / All our merchandise meets government specifications. It will satisfy the most particular individual. Immediate shipment can be made on everything / we manufacture. Send us your contract. Sincerely yours, (50)

_____

_____

_____

_____

_____

3. Dear Sir: Just a short time ago air-conditioning was considered a luxury. To have the comfort of an air / -conditioner in the home was very rare. Some offices and stores had this convenience but it has just been of / late that most new buildings are air-conditioned. In the warmer sections, most homes and cars are also

air-conditioned. / Our air-conditioners are priced so low that you can enjoy the comfort once available to very few. Sincerely yours, (80)

---

4. When applying for a new job, it is important that the first impression the employer has of you is a / good impression. You should be dressed in such a way that the employer will feel that you have good taste, / good judgment, and that you are neat in everything you do. You must wear a pleasant smile and extend a / kind word to assure him that you will get along with your fellow employees. You must answer all his questions / without hesitation and in a pleasant voice. If this is your first job, or if you have not worked for / some time, be sure to have the names and addresses of some people who know you well to give as / references. If you do not make a good first impression, you may not have the opportunity to demonstrate your ability. (140)

_____

_____

_____

_____

_____

_____

_____

5. Dear Mary: I must take the time to write and tell you of the amazing and interesting course I am / taking in school. It is a course in ABC Shorthand. After just a few hours of study, I am able / to take simple dictation. I have two more lessons to study before I complete all the theory. As soon as / I have learned all the rules, I will be able to take dictation on all types of material. At first, / my dictation speeds will be rather slow. With a little practice and a few more classes, I will be able / to take dictation from 80 to 100 words-a-minute. As soon as I am satisfied that I can / take dictation fast enough to pass a test, I will go out and apply for a job. I will first / go to one of the corporations or associations in the city. If I do not like the jobs they offer / me, I will then see what they have to offer in the government. It will be real fun to take / dictation from a company official or some administrator in the government. Taking shorthand gives an individual the opportunity to reach / a responsible position much faster. I am so pleased that I have learned this easy ABC Shorthand. I was sure / you would want to know it is easy and that you would want to learn it too. Very truly yours, (240)

_____

_____

_____

_____

6. Transcribe the following:

[handwritten shorthand text spanning six lines]

—l w de w—. i l b nssy f u l s—s
kpe nfo rg 9 u p8 mpy— + ne o—r
prl nfo u fe l b mp-l l s n mag
—s dsy. —s jb-k le l — adm pzz v
sa mnp + w m8 ck ec ndv z w
+pk z asn w—s og l b pmn—.
vlu,

HOMEWORK

LESSON VI

1. Dear Sir: We want to be fair with you but we cannot let you take advantage of us. We must / insist that you live up to our contract. The work must be finished on time, and it will be checked / to make sure that it is properly done. Sincerely, (50)

_____

_____

_____

_____

2. Gentlemen: We are fully aware of the problems we will meet in cancelling our contract with you. We do not / feel that this is a legal contract. Since you do not agree, it is evident that the matter will have / to be settled in court. Have your lawyer contact us if you wish to take legal action. Very truly yours, (60)

_____

_____

_____

_____

_____

3. Dear Sir: We have just received some new samples of rugs. They are made for use in reception rooms and / offices where traffic is heavy. These rugs are custom designed and can be made with your trademark as part / of the design. They can be made in any size you might want, even circular. If you need a really / nice rug for use where many of your customers walk, we would like to show you these samples. Yours truly, (80)

_____

_____

_____

_____

_____

_____

4. Dear Sir: After looking further into the matter we discussed in my office, I would advise you to seek the / services of a good lawyer. Since your contractor has not lived up to the terms of your agreement, indications are / that he does not intend to complete the work. It would be my advice to take action against him as / soon as possible. Some time ago I was taught a very costly lesson when one of the subcontractors working on / one of our jobs failed to do his work satisfactorily. I did not go to a lawyer promptly, and by / the time I took action, he had gone out of business. I had to pay out of my own pocket / to have the work finished satisfactorily. If you do not know a lawyer in whom you have complete confidence, I / will be glad to give you the names of several lawyers I know who are very competent, and who will / act in your best interest. Call me tonight. Yours truly, (170)

_____

_____

_____

_____

_____

_____

_____

5. Dear Madam: Thank you for your recent order for our number 102 bed. This is one of our / most popular items. Our circular offering this bed at a special sale price sold so many beds that we / have sold all of the number 102 beds we had. We expect a new shipment from the manufacturer / very shortly. As soon as this shipment arrives, we will fill your order. If you are in need of a / new bed right away, let us know and we will substitute our number 104 bed. If you prefer / the substitution, there will be no extra charge, and we promise that you will be fully satisfied. Very truly yours, (120)

6. Transcribe the following:

fu ppl rlz — l lcr r pbBl - sk
m8 mp— gu v ppl n — r lv. s nl —oz
w gu s n r rlys lu k f8, b —oz w
gu s n slkg + ppag f r fcr kre r
rsp l a ga xl— f r skss. n reg 8yo —
lv v fms ppl u l f — l m v — m
rknz — fk — l — r skss i d n a lg
p/ l — nspry, nkry — + nlg rsv fm
— r lcr. — s i — wd lcr r rpa f — r
Kby l — lv v — r Sd — . a lcr
ga8 r/ k fm — sl + nlg — l — a ma
n: sm sml wa klbu l — skss v
sm v — r Sd — .

NOTES

HOMEWORK

LESSON VII

1. Dear Sir: Until last month, your account has always been paid promptly. You are now 20 days late. We are / writing you because you have always paid on time before. Write and tell us why your payment is late. We / will try to help you if possible. Very truly yours, (50)

_____

_____

_____

_____

_____

2. Dear Sir: This is the time of the year to buy a new suit. Our new winter line has just / arrived, and we are selling our summer suits at a large discount. We still have a good selection of colors / and styles. Stop in and see us soon. You will be glad you did. We will look for you. Sincerely, (60)

_____

_____

_____

_____

_____

3. Dear Madam: One of your very dear friends suggested that we write and tell you about White Magic, the new / skin lotion that removes wrinkles and lines. This is possible because we use a new chemical that will draw your / skin tight. Many of our customers tell us that a two week treatment with White Magic does as good a /

job as plastic surgery. We also receive letters from women over forty who tell us that after trying this wonderful / lotion they have been mistaken for their own daughters. Because one of your friends has suggested that you could use / our product, and because we are sure that you will want it, we have sent a two weeks supply. When / you receive it, merely send us a check for $9.95 which is the full cost to / you. We would like to ask a favor. Please have a picture taken before you start the treatment and another / when you finish and send both pictures to us. We may use them in our national promotion campaign. Sincerely, (180)

4. Transcribe the following:

ds: m co r h lB glg — r mds zp rpdl b
sml lwn. w h ma a spx Sd v — s
pbm he l NSa lkg co. — u arny —
w — m sml b rliB lkg co w r nw
aB l gv Vme svs l ne lwn n V 300
me fm — s s. ull — s pn z w — Q
b s, l hz lan Q + ev W l ma dlvy
l sm v — z lwn. w — g u l le — s
nw svs. pz kl o s l hp u — nx le
u h a zp — g l ne lwn wa svs
hz b so n — pl. w l amz u. ul,

_____

_____

_____

_____

_____

_____

_____

_____

5. Nearly everyone would like to have a business of his own. It is because of this desire for independence that / we have become the most powerful and prosperous nation in the world. The first requirement for success in a small / business is ability. Ambition and the determination to see something through are also very important. Even with these qualities many / small businesses fail due to the lack of money. It is desirable to have a substantial reserve of money before / beginning your own business. Many of our large and most successful businesses have, nevertheless, been started with little / or no money in the bank. If other circumstances are favorable, lack of money should not stop you from opening / your own business. Many helpful books on this subject can be obtained from the Government Printing Office for very little. (140)

_____

_____

_____

_____

_____

_____

_____

_____

_____

_____

_____

_____

_____

6. Write the correct shorthand for the following words:

1. argue	_____	13. disagree	_____
2. badly	_____	14. entertain	_____
3. blasted	_____	15. hope	_____
4. bushel	_____	16. misery	_____
5. card	_____	17. misjudge	_____
6. chance	_____	18. shallow	_____
7. choice	_____	19. sinking	_____
8. chow	_____	20. stable	_____
9. circular	_____	21. subversive	_____
10. city	_____	22. watchful	_____
11. comment	_____	23. transmission	_____
12. counteract	_____	24. until	_____

PHRASING IN STENOSCRIPT ABC SHORTHAND

(Extracted from a manuscript on phraseology prepared by Paul Stokes)

Phrasing is used in all shorthand systems to increase the speed of experienced writers. You too, will find phrasing valuable to you in the writing of familiar and frequently used phrases.

Once you have mastered the theory of STENOSCRIPT ABC SHORTHAND and have learned to take dictation accurately, you will be able to apply the following principles to many phrases used in your daily dictation.

Phrasing in STENOSCRIPT ABC SHORTHAND is simple and logical. Following, as it does, a STANDARD WRITING PATTERN in connecting words, it is almost limitless in its application.

You will materially profit from your practice of phraseology. Ability to phrase is important to speed and writing comfort. Phrasing to shorthand, relatively speaking, is as important a mechanic as rhythm is to typewriting. For example, if while taking dictation, you encounter the common phrase — *Thank you for your letter,* the STENO-SCRIPT ABC SHORTHAND phrase outline would be written as follows:

Phrasing, or connected-line-writing, is a skill which can be attained only after diligent practice. The following formula, or practice routine, using the phrase indicated above, is offered as a suggested procedure:

Step 1.

Step 2.

Step 3.

Step 4.

Step 5.

Now, let us examine this phrase as written by an experienced STENOSCRIPT ABC SHORTHAND writer:

A sound rule to follow in developing phrase writing ability is to write only the shorthand for those words essential to suggesting the entire phrase, omitting the non-essential words (like a telegram).

Hear the sentence, follow the thought, and simultaneously keep pace with the dictator. Strive constantly to effect ease of writing and insist on a high-level — automatic writing style to assure easy transcription.

FREQUENTLY USED PHRASES

to me	*le*	I do not believe	*Idnblv*
to my	*lm*	we do not	*wdn*
to meet	*lme*	we do not believe	*wdnblv*
to mean	*lme*	they do not	*adn*
to know	*ln*	they do not know	*adnn*
to make	*lma*	you do not	*udn*
at once	*lws*	you do not know	*udnn*
it must be	*rmsb*	I had	*Ih*
it may be	*rmab*	he had	*eh*
at any	*lne*	they had	*ah*
at any time	*lnete*	we had	*wh*
in due course	*ndks*	you had	*uh*
in due time	*ndle*	was not	*zn*
to draw	*lda*	it was not	*izn*
what to do	*wtd*	he was not	*ezn*
I do not	*Idn*	it is not	*in*
I do not see	*Idns*	there is not	*rin*
I do not know	*Idnn*	at all	*ll*

69

of them	*v—m*	as you	*zu*
when the	*wn*	we are	*wr*
into the	*nl*	we will	*wl*
in reply	*nrpl*	we shall	*wzl*
on our	*or*	we can	*wk*
to go	*lg*	we are not	*wrn*
did not	*dn*	we will not	*wln*
to ask	*las*	we shall not	*wzln*
all of them	*lv—m*	we shall be	*wzlb*
we would	*wwd*	we have	*wh*
we should	*wzd*	we have been	*whb*
does not	*dzn*	we have not	*whn*
we must	*wms*	to see	*lc*
that they	*la*	to which	*lwc*
to keep	*lke*	to ship	*lzp*
which have	*wch*	to say	*lsa*
who have	*wh*	to honor	*lonr*
if you are	*iur*	to our	*lr*
are not	*rn*	to pay	*lpa*
we may	*wma*	to work	*lw*
with us	*w—s*	to place	*lpa*
will you	*lu*	as well as	*zlz*
through the	*u*	as good as	*zgdz*
for us	*fs*	as low as	*zloz*
over the	*v*	as much as	*zmcz*

70

as great as		he is	
as many as		of their	
have been able		is not	
would be able		of which	
should be able		to get	
will be able		to take	
on the		in his	
you are		if you will	
must be		that this	
should be		which is	
with the		on your (on you)	
if the		with that	
as to		from you (from your)	
at that		of its	
about the		he will	
to give		you would	
you know		to this	
of it		for the	
that is		to be	
in which		I have	
of these		from the	
more than		of this	
your letter		there are	
that is		you have	
you may		there is	

HOW TO GIVE DICTATION

After you have completed the seven theory lessons and start dictation, you must take practice dictation every day. This is extremely important as it is your only means of attaining your speed goal.

You must work continuously for a higher speed. To increase your speed in taking dictation will require as much effort as is required to increase speed in typing. You must continually attempt to take dictation at a speed somewhat higher than your ability.

When you are able to take dictation at a given speed with only 3 to 5 errors, it is time to increase the dictation speed 10 words a minute. Gradually you will increase your ability to coordinate your hearing, thinking and writing powers.

The person whom you select for a dictator will enjoy his part in your training if he really wants to help you. You will find, however that an inexperienced dictator will not speak evenly or accurately. He may even find himself pacing you because it is tempting to a dictator not to leave you behind. The dictator should challenge you by increasing his speed as you progress.

Your first speed goal is 60 words a minute. The average person writes longhand at approximately 40 words a minute. With the added burden of putting the theory into actual practice, you will find that you probably cannot take the dictation correctly at 60 words a minute the first time you try. Nevertheless, after five or ten one-minute speed tests you will gain accuracy in shorthand and attain speed. When you do attain the speed and are making only 3 to 5 errors, you should increase your speed goal to 70 words a minute and so on at each speed level.

The aim in all shorthand systems is to reduce your writing to a minimum and to increase your ability to write more words a minute. In this system your writing is reduced approximately two-thirds and as you become completely familiar with the theory, assuming your average longhand speed is 40 words a minute, you will be able to take dictation at the rate of about 120 words a minute.

The only way to accomplish your purpose is to observe regular study hours. Be honest with yourself — any worth-while task takes time.

Whenever you have a letter in your dictation book that does not have enough words to fill the required time, use a part of the next letter. Do not include addresses in dictation because they are not usually included in the word count found at the end of the letter. Know how your dictation book is organized. Read the preface and the instructions.

Do not skip from one part of the dictation book to another because the letters are put in a sequence which is for your benefit. If you follow this procedure, you will build your shorthand vocabulary gradually and surely and increase your speed more effectively.

Use a dictation pad with a line down the center. Write to the center line all the way down the first column and then down the second.

After taking each speed test, have the dictator read back the longhand slowly so that you may correct any errors. This is important.

Use a stop-watch with a second hand or an ordinary clock with a second hand. It is of utmost importance that you time yourself accurately. During an examination for a job, you may be completely lost if you have not been strict about timing your dictation speed.

Always write as fast as you can and get your shorthand as accurate as possible. Do not fight difficult words. It is better to omit words that are hard for you. You will learn more difficult words in time. Concentrating on a single word during dictation could result in your losing a whole sentence.

Letters and articles in this book, as well as those in most dictation books, are divided into groups of 20 words. Use the following table to determine correct dictation speed.

Words a Minute	Dictate Each Group of 20 Words In
50	24 seconds
60	20 "
70	17 "
80	15 "
90	13 "
100	12 "
110	11 "
120	10 "

ADAPTING STENOSCRIPT ABC SHORTHAND TO YOUR JOB

Most shorthand courses will not prepare you for any particular type of business, but there is a way to adapt this shorthand to any business in which you need to use it.

You have learned that this system uses 11 capital letters to represent words. This leaves 15 capital letters which you may utilize to represent the 15 most frequently occurring words in your business. For example, if you are with an insurance company, capital **L** should be *liability* because that word occurs very frequently in the insurance business.

When you are employed, list what you consider to be the high-frequency words in your business and assign a capital letter to each of the 15 most-frequently occurring words. This is an additional speed-builder.

Listed below are those capital letters which you may utilize as suggested above. Fill in the blanks with words useful to you.

A _____   L _____

B _____   P _____

C _____   Q _____

E _____   R _____

G _____   S _____

H _____   T _____

J _____   X _____

   _____   Z _____

TRANSCRIPTION TIPS

Stenographers are no better than their ability to transcribe their shorthand notes accurately. STENOSCRIPT ABC SHORTHAND is probably the easiest to transcribe of all shorthand systems. The following "tips" may, however, provide you with more rapid transcription of your STENOSCRIPT ABC SHORTHAND notes.

(a) In STENOSCRIPT ABC SHORTHAND you **do not** write a vowel within a <u>base</u> word. You do, however, write vowels within a compound word or derivative. When you see a vowel written within a word this indicates that the vowel ends or begins a base word and that a prefix or suffix has been added to the base word. For easy transcription you always transcribe the base word first and then add the prefix or suffix. Examples:

In the first word above if you transcribe only as far as **pa,** you get the base word **pay** and find that by adding the suffix you get the word **payment.** The second word transcribed through **lo** gives you the base word **low** and adding the suffix gives you the word **lower.** The other words transcribed give you first **apply,** then **appliance; like,** then **likely; broke,** then **broken.** In the last word you transcribe the word **act** and add the prefix **re** to get the word **react.**

REMEMBER: Anytime a vowel appears within a word it is the beginning or end of a base word and the BASE WORD should be transcribed first. It is then easy to get the rest of the word.

(b) The following chart contains <u>all</u> possible vowel-consonant-vowel endings to words. It is used to assist in transcription when a shorthand for a word ends in a vowel and you cannot immediately transcribe it. Reference to this chart will give you the word fast and accurately. For example if you could not immediately transcribe the word

in the following sentence you would go to the **e column** of the chart and find that the word could only be **feel.**

and the sentence reads: **The boy does not feel well.** If the word in question ended in the vowel **a** you would go to the **a column,** etc.

76

The following is a list of all possible ending-sounds for words where accentuated vowel rule has been used.

(a--)	(e--)	(i--)	(o--)	(u--)
abe	ebe	ibe	obe	ube
ace	ece	ice	oce	uce
ade	ede	ide	ode	ude
afe	efe	ife	ofe	ufe
ake	eke	ike	oke	uke
ale	ele	ile	ole	ule
ame	eme	ime	ome	ume
ane	ene	ine	one	une
ape	epe	ipe	ope	upe
are	ere	ire	ore	ure
ase	ese	ise	ose	use
ate	ete	ite	ote	ute

Many STENOSCRIPT ABC SHORTHAND writers have found it convenient to type this chart on a card and attach it to the desk where they transcribe so that it will be available for easy reference.

NOTES

STENOSCRIPT ABC SHORTHAND DICTIONARY

PART I

General Business Dictionary — Approximately 5,000 of the Most Used Words in Business Correspondence.

NOTES

GENERAL BUSINESS DICTIONARY

Word	Shorthand	Word	Shorthand
a	*a*	acceptable	*aksp6*
abandoned	*abn*	acceptance	*aksp,*
ability	*aB,*	accepted	*aksp,*
able	*aB*	accepting	*akspg*
abnormal	*abnml*	accessory	*akssy*
about	*abwl*	accident	*aksd*
above	*abv*	accidental	*aksd l*
absence	*abs,*	accommodate	*akmda*
absolutely	*abslul*	accompany	*ac*
abstract	*abSk*	accomplish	*ac*
abundance	*abs*	accord	*ak*
abuse	*aby*	accordance	*ak'*
academic	*akdmk*	according	*ak g*
accelerated	*akslra*	accost	*akS*
accept	*aksp*	account	*ak*

accountant	*ak*	addresses	*ads*
accounted	*ak*	adds	*ad*
accounting	*ak g*	adequate	*aql*
accrue	*aku*	adequately	*aqll*
accumulate	*aqmla*	adjacent	*ajs*
accumulated	*aqmla*	adjudge	*ayy*
accuracy	*abrc*	adjust	*ajs*
accurate	*akrl*	adjusted	*ajs*
accustomed	*akSm*	adjusting	*ajSg*
achieved	*acv*	adjustment	*ajs*
achievement	*acv*	administrate	*adm*
acknowledge	*ak*	administration	*adm*
acquaint	*aq*	administrative	*adm*
acquire	*aqu*	administrator	*adm*
acre	*akr*	admission	*amy*
acreage	*akry*	admit	*aml*
across	*aks*	admitted	*aml*
act	*ak*	adopt	*adp*
action	*akj*	adopted	*adp*
active	*akv*	advance	*avs*
actual	*aku*	advanced	*avs*
adding	*adg*	advancement	*avs*
addition	*adj*	advantage	*av j*
address	*ads*	advertise	*avlj*
addressee	*adse*	advertised	*avlj*

advertisement		agent	
advertisers		ages	
advertising		aggregate	
advice		aggression	
advisable		aggressive	
advise		ago	
advised		agree	
adviser		agreed	
advising		agreement	
advisory		agriculture	
affairs		ahead	
affect		aid	
affected		aim	
affecting		air	
affiliated		aircraft	
afford		air-conditioned	
afforded		air-conditioner	
afraid		air-conditioners	
after		air-conditioning	
afternoon		airmail	
again		airport	
against		album	
age		alert	
agency		all	
agencies		allied	

allocated	*alka*	amendment	*a*
allocation	*alkj*	American	*amkn*
allotment	*all*	ammunition	*amny*
allow	*alw*	among	*amg*
allowable	*alwB*	amortized	*am Z*
allowance	*alwy*	amount	*am*
allowed	*alw*	amounting	*am g*
allowing	*alwg*	ample	*ampl*
alloy	*aly*	amply	*ampl*
almost	*lmS*	an	*a*
alone	*alo*	analysis	*anlss*
along	*alg*	analyze	*anlz*
already	*lrd*	and	*a* OR +
also	*lo*	anesthetic	*ans lk*
altered	*alr*	angel	*anjl*
although	*l o*	animal	*anml*
aluminum	*almnm*	announce	*anuy*
always	*lwz*	anniversary	*anvsy*
am	*m*	announced	*anuy*
amaze	*amz*	announcement	*anuz*
amazing	*amzg*	announcing	*anuzg*
amazingly	*amzgl*	annoy	*any*
ambition	*amby*	annoyance	*anyp*
ambulance	*ambly*	annual	*anl*
amended	*a*	annually	*anll*

84

Word	Shorthand
annuities	*any*
annum	*anm*
another	*aor*
answer	*ansr*
answered	*ansr*
answering	*ansrg*
anticipate	*anlspa*
anticipated	*anlspa*
antitrust	*anlts*
anxious	*aqx*
any	*ne*
anybody	*nebd*
anyone	*newn*
anything	*ne g*
anytime	*neti*
anyway	*newa*
anywhere	*newa*
apart	*ap*
apartment	*ap*
apparel	*apl*
apparent	*ap*
apparently	*apl*
appeal	*ape*
appear	*ape*
appearance	*apes*

Word	Shorthand
appeared	*ape*
appearing	*apeg*
appendix	*ap x*
appliance	*apy*
applicable	*apkb*
applicant	*apk*
application	*apky*
applied	*api*
apply	*api*
applying	*apig*
appoint	*apy*
appointment	*apy*
appraisal	*apzl*
appreciate	*ap*
appreciated	*ap*
appreciation	*ap*
approach	*apc*
appropriate	*appa*
appropriation	*appy*
approval	*apvl*
approve	*apv*
approved	*apv*
approximate	*apx*
approximately	*apx*
arches	*rc*

architectural	*rklkcl*	ask	*as*
are	*r*	asked	*as*
area	*ara*	asking	*asg*
argue	*rgu*	aspects	*aspk*
arguments	*rgu*	assemble	*asmß*
arise	*arz*	assembled	*asmß*
arm	*rml*	assert	*as*
armed	*rm*	assessments	*ass*
army	*rme*	assets	*asl*
around	*ar*	assign	*asu*
arrange	*arng*	assigned	*asu*
arranged	*arng*	assignment	*asu*
arrangement	*arng*	assist	*asl*
arranging	*arnga*	assistance	*asl*
array	*ara*	assistant	*asl*
arrival	*arvl*	assisting	*aslg*
arrive	*arv*	associate	*asn*
arrived	*arv*	associated	*asn*
arrives	*arv*	association	*asn*
arriving	*arvg*	associations	*asn*
art	*/*	assortment	*as*
article	*kl*	assume	*asu*
artists	*8*	assumed	*asu*
as	*z*	assumption	*asmy*
aside	*asu*	assurance	*azuy*

assure	*azu*	audience	*ads*
assured	*azu*	audit	*adl*
assuring	*azug*	auditing	*adlg*
at	*l*	auditor	*adbr*
ate	*al*	auditorium	*adlrm*
atmosphere	*almsfe*	author	*a r*
attach	*alc*	authority	*a ry*
attached	*alc*	authorization	*a rry*
attaching	*alcg*	authorized	*a rry*
attachment	*alcl*	auto	*alo*
attack	*alk*	automatic	*alomlk*
attain	*ala*	automatically	*alomlkl*
attempt	*almp*	automobile	*alomb*
attempted	*almp*	automotive	*alomv*
attempting	*almpg*	availability	*avab*
attend	*al*	available	*avab*
attendance	*al*	average	*avj*
attended	*al*	averaged	*avj*
attending	*al g*	aviation	*avj*
attention	*aln*	avoid	*avyd*
attentive	*alnv*	avoided	*avyd*
attic	*alk*	await	*ava*
attitude	*allu*	awaiting	*avag*
attorney	*alne*	award	*a*
attractive	*alkv*	awarded	*a*

87

aware	_awa_	bath	_b_
away	_awa_	battery	_bly_
awful	_ay_	be	_b_
babies	_bb_	beams	_be_
back	_bk_	bear	_ba_
backed	_bk_	beat	_be_
backward	_bk_	beautiful	_bly_
backing	_bkg_	beauty	_bt_
bad	_bd_	beaver	_bvr_
badly	_bdl_	became	_bk_
bag	_bg_	because	_bkz_
balance	_bl_	become	_bk_
balanced	_bl_	becoming	_bk_
bales	_ba_	bed	_bd_
ball	_bl_	bedrooms	_bdru_
ballot	_bll_	been	_b_
band	_b_	beetles	_bll_
bank	_bg_	before	_bf_
banker	_bgr_	beg	_bg_
banking	_bgg_	began	_bg_
banquet	_bnql_	begin	_bg_
base	_ba_	beginning	_bg_
basement	_ba_	begun	_bg_
basic	_bsk_	behalf	_bhf_
basis	_bss_	behind	_bh_

88

Word	Shorthand	Word	Shorthand
being		billing	
belief		billion	
beliefs		bills	
believe		binder	
believed		binding	
belong		bird	
belongs		birth	
below		birthday	
belt		bit	
beneath		bitten	
beneficial		black	
beneficiary		blank	
benefit		blanket	
besides		blind	
best		block	
better		blood	
between		blotter	
beyond		blow	
bible		blue	
bid		board	
bidder		boat	
big		body	
bigger		bond	
biggest		bonding	
bill		bone	

bonus	*bns*	break	*ba*
book	*bk*	breakfast	*bkfs*
bookkeeping	*bkkeg*	bribe	*bi*
booklet	*bkll*	brief	*be*
books	*bk*	briefly	*bel*
bookstore	*bkSo*	bright	*bi*
boom	*bu*	bring	*bg*
boost	*bs*	bringing	*bgg*
booth	*b*	broad	*bd*
born	*bn*	broadcast	*bdks*
borrow	*bro*	brochure	*bzu*
borrowed	*bro*	broke	*bo*
both	*b*	broken	*bon*
bottle	*bll*	broker	*bor*
bottom	*blm*	brokerage	*bory*
bought	*bl*	brother	*bu*
bound	*b*	brought	*bl*
boundary	*by*	brown	*bun*
box	*bx*	brush	*bz*
boxing	*bxg*	buff	*bf*
boy	*by*	build	*bd*
bracket	*bbkl*	building	*bdg*
branch	*bnc*	buildings	*bdg*
brand	*b*	built	*bl*
brass	*bs*	bulletin	*blln*

90

burden	*bn*
bureau	*bro*
bus	*bs*
bushels	*bx*
business	*bz*
businesses	*bz*
businessman	*bzmn*
busy	*bz*
but	*b*
butane	*bla*
butter	*blr*
buy	*b*
buying	*bg*
by	*b*
bylaws	*bla*
cab	*kb*
cabinet	*kbnl*
cable	*kB*
cage	*kj*
calamity	*klmy*
calculating	*kglag*
calendar	*kl d*
call	*kl*
called	*kl*
calling	*klg*

came	*k*
camp	*km*
campaign	*kmpa*
campus	*kmps*
can	*k*
cancel	*knsl*
cancellation	*knsly*
cancelling	*knsly*
cancer	*knsr*
candidate	*kndda*
cane	*ka*
cannot	*kn*
cans	*k*
canvass	*knvs*
cap	*kp*
capable	*kpB*
capacity	*kps*
capital	*kpll*
captain	*kpln*
captioned	*kpj*
car	*kr*
carbon	*kbn*
card	*k*
care	*ka*
career	*kre*

91

careers	_kre_	caught	_kt_
carefree	_kafe_	cause	_kz_
careful	_kdy_	cease	_se_
carefully	_kay_	cedar	_cdr_
cargo	_kgo_	ceiling	_seg_
carload	_krlo_	cellar	_slr_
carpet	_kpl_	cement	_s_
carriage	_ky_	cent	_s_
carried	_ky_	censor	_snsr_
carrier	_kyr_	center	_s r_
carry	_ky_	central	_s l_
carrying	_kyg_	century	_s y_
cars	_kr_	certain	_s n_
carton	_k n_	certainly	_s nl_
case	_ka_	certificate	_sfkt_
cash	_kz_	certification	_sfky_
cashier	_kre_	certified	_sfi_
cast	_ks_	certifying	_sfyg_
casualty	_kxl_	chain	_ca_
catalog	_kllg_	chair	_ca_
catastrophe	_klSe_	chairman	_camn_
catch	_kc_	challenge	_clny_
category	_klgy_	chamber	_cmbr_
cater	_klr_	chance	_cs_
cattle	_kll_	change	_cny_

92

chapter	*cphr*	choice	*cys*
character	*krkr*	choir	*qi*
charge	*cy*	choose	*cz*
charged	*cy*	chop	*cp*
charitable	*chtb*	chopped	*cp*
charity	*cry*	chorus	*krs*
chart	*c*	chosen	*czn*
charter	*cr*	Christian	*ksn*
chattel	*cll*	Christmas	*ksms*
cheap	*ce*	church	*cc*
cheaper	*cer*	cider	*sdr*
check	*ck*	cigar	*sgr*
checked	*ck*	cipher	*sfr*
checking	*ckg*	circle	*cl*
checkup	*ckp*	circuit	*cl*
cheer	*ce*	circular	*clr*
cheese	*cz*	circulation	*cly*
chemical	*kmkl*	circumflex	*cflx*
chemicals	*kmkl*	circumspect	*cspk*
cherry	*cy*	circumstances	*cs*
chest	*cs*	circumvent	*cv*
chief	*ce*	cite	*si*
child	*cd*	cities	*ss*
children	*cdn*	citizen	*slzn*
chocolate	*ckll*	citrus	*sls*

city	*Sy*	clinical	*knkl*
civic	*svk*	close	*ky*
civil	*svl*	closed	*kz*
civilian	*svln*	closely	*kol*
claim	*ka*	closing	*kzg*
claims	*ka*	cloth	*kl*
clarification	*krfkj*	clothing	*k g*
clarify	*klfi*	club	*kb*
class	*ks*	coach	*kc*
classes	*ks*	coal	*ko*
classification	*ksfkj*	coast	*ks*
classified	*ksfi*	coated	*ko*
classroom	*ksru*	code	*ko*
clean	*ke*	coffee	*kfe*
cleaned	*ke*	cold	*kd*
cleaner	*ker*	collateral	*klll*
cleaning	*keg*	collect	*klk*
clear	*ke*	collected	*klk*
clearance	*key*	collecting	*klkg*
cleared	*ke*	collection	*klkj*
clearly	*kel*	collectors	*klkr*
clerk	*k*	college	*klj*
clever	*kvr*	color	*klr*
client	*k*	colored	*klr*
clinic	*knk*	colorful	*klrj*

94

colors	*klr*
column	*klm*
comb	*ko*
combat	*kbl*
combination	*kbny*
combined	*kbi*
come	*k*
comes	*k*
comfort	*kf*
comfortable	*kfb*
coming	*k*
commander	*k r*
commanding	*k g*
commence	*kmy*
commencement	*kms*
comments	*k*
commerce	*kms*
commercial	*kmx*
commission	*kmy*
commissioner	*kmjr*
commitment	*kml*
committee	*kmk*
commodity	*kmd*
common	*kmn*
commonly	*kmnl*

commonwealth	*kmnw*
communicate	*kmnka*
communication	*kmnkj*
Communism	*kmnzm*
Communist	*kmns*
community	*kmny*
compact	*kpk*
companies	*co*
companion	*kpnn*
company	*co*
comparable	*kpB*
compare	*kpa*
compared	*kpa*
comparing	*kpag*
comparison	*kpasn*
compartment	*kp*
compass	*kps*
compel	*kpl*
compelled	*kpl*
compensation	*kpnsj*
compete	*kpe*
competent	*kpl*
competing	*kpeg*
competition	*kplj*
competitive	*kplv*

95

compilation	*kpely*	conclusive	*kksv*
compiled	*kpi*	concrete	*kke*
complete	*kpe*	condemn	*kdm*
completed	*kpe*	condense	*kds*
completely	*kpel*	condensed	*kds,*
completing	*kpeg*	condition	*kdj*
completion	*kpj*	conditioning	*kdjg*
compliance	*kpis*	conduct	*kdk*
complicated	*kpka*	conducted	*kdk*
compliment	*kp*	conducting	*kdkg*
comply	*kpi*	conference	*kfs*
composed	*kpz*	confidence	*kfds*
compound	*kp*	confident	*kfd*
comprehensive	*kphv*	confidential	*kfdnx*
comptroller	*kllr*	confined	*kfi*
computed	*kpu*	confinement	*kfi*
computing	*kpug*	confining	*kfig*
concentrate	*ksnla*	confirm	*kfm*
concern	*ksn*	confirmation	*kfmj*
concerned	*ksn*	confirming	*kfmg*
concerning	*ksng*	conflict	*kflk*
concise	*ksi*	conflicting	*kflkg*
conclaves	*kkv*	confronted	*kf*
conclude	*kku*	confused	*kfz*
conclusion	*kkj*	confusion	*kfj*

congress		constitutional	
congressional		construct	
congressman		construction	
connected		constructive	
connection		consult	
conscientious		consultant	
consecutive		consultation	
consent		consumer	
consequently		contact	
conservation		contacted	
conservative		contacting	
considerable		contain	
consider		contained	
consideration		containing	
considered		contemplate	
considering		contemplated	
consist		contemplating	
consistently		content	
consisting		contest	
consolidated		contingent	
consolidation		continue	
constant		contract	
constantly		contracting	
constitute		contractor	
constitution		contradict	

contrary	*kly*	corporations	*crp*
contribute	*klbu*	correct	*krk*
contributed	*klbu*	correcting	*krkg*
contributing	*klbug*	correction	*krkj*
contribution	*Kbj*	correctly	*krkl*
control	*klo*	correspondence	*krsp,*
controllers	*klor*	corresponding	*krsp g*
controversy	*Kvc*	corrosion	*kry*
convenience	*kvny*	corrugated	*krga*
convenient	*kvn*	cost	*ks*
convention	*kvny*	costly	*ksl*
conversation	*kvsj*	cottage	*kly*
convert	*kv*	cotton	*kln*
conviction	*kvkj*	could	*kd*
convince	*ky*	count	*k*
convinced	*kvs*	counter	*K*
cool	*ku*	counteract	*Kak*
copy	*kp*	counterfeit	*Kfl*
cord	*k*	country	*k y*
cordial	*kjl*	county	*k e*
cordially	*kjll*	couple	*kpl*
corn	*kn*	coupon	*gpn*
corner	*knr*	courage	*kry*
corporate	*Crp*	course	*ks*
corporation	*Crp*	court	*k*

98

cover	*kvr*	curricula	*krkla*
coverage	*kvrj*	curriculum	*krklm*
covered	*kvr*	curious	*gr*
covering	*kvrg*	curtail	*kla*
cow	*kw*	custom	*ksm*
creak	*ke*	customary	*ksmy*
cream	*ke*	customer	*ksmr*
created	*ka*	cut	*kt*
create	*ka*	cutting	*ktg*
credentials	*kdny*	daily	*dl*
credit	*kdt*	dairy	*dy*
credited	*kdt*	dam	*dm*
crediting	*kdtg*	damage	*dmj*
crime	*kr*	damaged	*dmj*
criminal	*kmnl*	damaging	*dmjg*
critic	*klk*	dance	*d,*
critical	*klkl*	dancing	*dg*
crop	*kp*	danger	*djr*
cross	*ks*	dangerous	*dnjrs*
crude	*ku*	dark	*dr*
cruel	*ku*	data	*dla*
cure	*ku*	date	*da*
currency	*krnc*	dated	*da*
current	*kr*	dating	*dag*
currently	*krl*	daughters	*dtr*

99

dawn	*dn*	deduct	*ddk*
day	*D*	deducted	*ddk*
days	*D*	deductible	*ddkB*
dead	*dd*	deduction	*ddkj*
deadline	*ddl*	deed	*de*
deal	*de*	deem	*de*
dealer	*der*	deep	*de*
dealings	*deg*	deeply	*del*
dean	*de*	deer	*de*
dear	*de*	defeated	*dfe*
death	*d*	defective	*dfkv*
debit	*dbl*	defense	*df*
debt	*dl*	defer	*dfr*
deceased	*dse*	deferred	*dfr*
decide	*dsi*	defiance	*df*
decided	*dsi*	defined	*df*
deciding	*dsig*	definite	*dfnl*
decision	*dsj*	definitely	*dfnll*
decline	*dki*	definitions	*dfnj*
declined	*dki*	defy	*df*
decontrol	*dklo*	degree	*dge*
decrease	*dke*	delay	*dla*
decreased	*dke*	delayed	*dla*
dedicated	*ddka*	delaying	*dlag*
dedication	*ddkj*	delegates	*dlga*

100

delete	*dle*	deposited	*dpzt*
delighted	*dli*	depreciable	*dpzB*
deliver	*dlvr*	depreciation	*dpzy*
delivered	*dlvr*	derive	*drv*
delivery	*dlvy*	derived	*drv*
deluxe	*dlx*	describe	*dkr*
demand	*d*	describing	*dkrg*
demanded	*d*	description	*dkpy*
democratic	*dmklk*	descriptive	*dkpv*
demonstrate	*dmnSa*	deserves	*dzv*
demonstrated	*dmnSa*	design	*dzr*
demonstrating	*dmnSag*	designate	*dzgna*
demonstration	*dmnSj*	designated	*dzgna*
denomination	*dnmny*	designed	*dzr*
dental	*dl*	desirable	*dzrB*
dentistry	*dSy*	desire	*dzr*
departmental	*dp*	desired	*dzr*
departure	*dp*	desiring	*dzrg*
depend	*dp*	desk	*ds*
dependable	*dpB*	despite	*dpr*
dependent	*dp*	destination	*dtny*
depending	*dpg*	destitute	*dtu*
depleted	*dpd*	destroy	*dSy*
deport	*dp*	destruction	*dSky*
depositary	*dpzty*	detachable	*dtcB*

detail	_dla_	difference	_dfr,_
detailed	_dla_	different	_dfr_
detect	_dīk_	difficult	_dfkl_
detective	_dlkv_	digest	_djS_
determination	_dlmny_	dimensions	_dmny_
determine	_dlmn_	dining	_dıg_
determined	_dlmn_	dinner	_dnr_
determining	_dlmng_	direct	_drk_
detest	_dlS_	directed	_drk_
develop	_dvlp_	direction	_drkj_
developed	_dvlp_	directly	_drkl_
developing	_dvlpg_	director	_drkr_
development	_dvlp_	directory	_drky_
device	_dvı_	disability	_dBy_
devious	_dvx_	disabled	_dB_
devote	_dvo_	disagree	_dage_
devoted	_dvo_	disappoint	_dapy_
devotion	_dvj_	disaster	_dSr_
dials	_dı_	disband	_db_
diameter	_dmlr_	discard	_dk_
dictated	_dkla_	discharge	_dcj_
dictation	_dklj_	discharged	_dcj_
did	_d_	discomfort	_dkf_
die	_dı_	discontinued	_dklnu_
differ	_dfr_	discount	_dk_

Word	Shorthand	Word	Shorthand
discover	*dkvr*	distributor	*dlbur*
discovered	*dkvr*	district	*dlk*
discuss	*dks*	distrust	*dlS*
discussed	*dks*	disturb	*dlb*
discussing	*dksg*	diversion	*dvj*
discussion	*dkj*	divided	*dvi*
disease	*dzz*	dividend	*dvd*
dishes	*dz*	divinity	*dvn*
dismissed	*dms*	division	*dvj*
disorder	*do*	divisional	*dvjl*
display	*dpa*	do	*d*
displayed	*dpa*	doctor	*dr* OR *dkh*
displaying	*dpag*	does	*dz*
disposal	*dpzl*	dog	*dg*
dispose	*dpz*	doing	*d*
disposing	*dpzg*	dollar	*dlr*
disposition	*dpzj*	domestic	*dmSk*
distance	*dl*	dominance	*dmns*
distant	*dl*	donation	*dnj*
distilled	*dll*	done	*d*
distinctive	*dlgv*	door	*do*
distribute	*dlbu*	dot	*dl*
distributed	*dlbu*	double	*dB*
distributing	*dlbug*	doubled	*dB*
distribution	*dlbj*	doubt	*dwl*

Word	Shorthand	Word	Shorthand
down	*dwn*	dues	*d*
doze	*dz*	duke	*du*
dozen	*dzn*	dummy	*dme*
draft	*df*	dungarees	*dgre*
draw	*da*	duplicate	*dpka*
drawer	*dar*	duplicated	*dpka*
drawing	*dag*	duplicating	*dpkag*
drawn	*dan*	duplication	*dpkj*
dread	*dd*	durable	*drb*
dressed	*ds*	during	*drg*
dressings	*dsg*	duty	*dl*
drink	*dg*	each	*ec*
drinks	*dg*	eager	*egr*
drive	*dv*	ear	*er*
driver	*dvr*	earlier	*elr*
driving	*dvg*	earliest	*els*
drop	*dp*	early	*el*
dropped	*dp*	earn	*en*
dropping	*dpg*	earned	*en*
drug	*dg*	earnestly	*ensl*
druggist	*dgs*	earnings	*eng*
drum	*dm*	earth	*el*
dry	*di*	earthquake	*e ga*
drying	*dig*	easier	*ezr*
due	*d*	easily	*ezl*

104

east	*E*	effort	
Easter	*Er*	egg	*eg*
Eastern	*En*	either	*e r*
easy	*ez*	elect	*elk*
eat	*el*	elected	*elk*
eaten	*eln*	election	*elky*
eating	*elg*	electric	*elkk*
economic	*eknmk*	electrical	*elkkl*
economical	*eknmkl*	electricity	*elks,*
economy	*eknme*	element	*l*
edge	*ey*	elementary	*l y*
edging	*eyg*	eligible	*lyd*
edition	*edy*	eliminate	*elmna*
editor	*edr*	eliminated	*elmna*
editorial	*edrl*	eliminating	*elmnag*
educate	*edka*	elimination	*elmny*
educated	*edka*	else	*ls*
education	*edky*	elsewhere	*lswa*
educational	*edkjl*	embezzle	*mlyl*
effect	*fk*	emergency	*mjnc*
effective	*fkv*	emphasis	*mfss*
effectively	*fkvl*	emphasize	*mfsz*
efficiency	*fync*	employ	*mpiy*
efficient	*fy*	employed	*mpiy*
efficiently	*fyl*	employee	*mpiye*

105

employer	*mpyr*	engine	*nyn*
employing	*mpyg*	engineer	*nyne*
employment	*mpy*	engineering	*nyneg*
enable	*nb*	English	*egz*
enabling	*nBg*	enjoy	*nyy*
enact	*nak*	enjoyable	*nyyB*
enclose	*nkz*	enjoyed	*nyy*
enclosed	*nkz*	enjoying	*nyyg*
enclosing	*nkzg*	enjoyment	*nyy*
enclosure	*nkzu*	enlisted	*nls*
encourage	*nkry*	enlistment	*nls*
encouragement	*nkry*	enough	*enf*
encouraging	*nkryg*	enrich	*nrc*
end		enroll	*nro*
endeavor	*ndvr*	enrolled	*nro*
ended		enrollment	*nro*
ending	*g*	ensuing	*nsug*
endorse	*nds*	enter	*n*
endorsed	*nds*	entered	*n*
endorsement	*nds*	entering	*ng*
endurance	*nduy*	enterprise	*npz*
endure	*ndu*	entertaining	*ntag*
enemy	*nme*	entertainment	*nta*
energy	*nrg*	entire	*nti*
engaged	*ngj*	entirely	*ntil*

entirety		estimating	
entitle		even	
entitled		evening	
entitles		event	
entrance		eventually	
entry		ever	
envelope		every	
enviable		everybody	
equal		everyday	
equally		everyone	
equipment		everything	
equipped		everywhere	
equitable		evidence	
equivalent		evidenced	
error		evident	
especially		evidently	
essential		exact	
establish		exactly	
established		examination	
establishing		examine	
establishment		examined	
estate		examining	
esteemed		example	
estimate		exceed	
estimated		exceeded	

exceeding	*[shorthand]*	existing	*[shorthand]*
excellent	*[shorthand]*	expand	*[shorthand]*
except	*[shorthand]*	expanding	*[shorthand]*
excepting	*[shorthand]*	expansion	*[shorthand]*
exception	*[shorthand]*	expect	*[shorthand]*
exceptional	*[shorthand]*	expected	*[shorthand]*
excess	*[shorthand]*	expecting	*[shorthand]*
excessive	*[shorthand]*	expedite	*[shorthand]*
exchangeable	*[shorthand]*	expenditures	*[shorthand]*
exchange	*[shorthand]*	expense	*[shorthand]*
exchanged	*[shorthand]*	expensive	*[shorthand]*
excise	*[shorthand]*	experience	*[shorthand]*
exciting	*[shorthand]*	experienced	*[shorthand]*
excluded	*[shorthand]*	expert	*[shorthand]*
exclusive	*[shorthand]*	experts	*[shorthand]*
execute	*[shorthand]*	expiration	*[shorthand]*
executed	*[shorthand]*	expire	*[shorthand]*
executive	*[shorthand]*	explain	*[shorthand]*
exempt	*[shorthand]*	explained	*[shorthand]*
exemption	*[shorthand]*	explaining	*[shorthand]*
exhausted	*[shorthand]*	explanation	*[shorthand]*
exhaustive	*[shorthand]*	explanatory	*[shorthand]*
exhibit	*[shorthand]*	export	*[shorthand]*
exist	*[shorthand]*	exposition	*[shorthand]*
existence	*[shorthand]*	express	*[shorthand]*

expressed		fails	
expressing		fair	
expression		fairly	
extend		faith	
extended		faithful	
extending		fake	
extension		fall	
extent		fame	
extra		familiar	
extreme		familiarize	
extremely		families	
eye		family	
fabric		famous	
face		fan	
facilitate		fancy	
facilities		far	
facility		fare	
facing		farm	
fact		farmer	
factor		farming	
factory		farther	
factual		fashion	
faculty		fashionable	
fail		fast	
failed		faster	

fatalities		fence	
fate		fertilizers	
father		few	
fault		field	
favor		fight	
favorable		fighting	
favorably		figure	
favored		figured	
favorite		file	
fear		filed	
feature		filing	
featured		fill	
features		filled	
featuring		fillers	
federal		filling	
fee		film	
feed		final	
feeding		finality	
feel		finally	
feeling		finance	
fees		financial	
feet		financing	
fellow		find	
fellowship		finding	
felt		fine	

110

finest		foil	
finish		folder	
finished		folding	
finishing		folks	
fire		follow	
firm		followed	
firmly		following	
first		food	
fiscal		foot	
fish		football	
fishing		for	
fit		forbid	
fitting		force	
fix		forced	
fixed		forecast	
fixture		foreclosure	
flashings		foreign	
flat		foremost	
flavor		forest	
fleet		forever	
flood		forget	
floor		form	
flow		formal	
fluid		former	
flush		formula	

forth		friend	
forthcoming		friends	
fortunate		friendly	
fortunately		friendship	
forum		from	
forward		front	
forwarded		frozen	
forwarding		fruit	
found		frying	
foundation		fudge	
framework		fuel	
franchise		fulfill	
frank		fulfillment	
frankly		full	
fraternally		fullest	
freak		full-time	
free		fully	
freedom		fun	
freeze		funny	
freight		function	
frequency		fund	
frequent		fundamental	
frequently		funeral	
fresh		fur	
freshman		furnish	

furnished		gentlemen	
furnishing		genuine	
furniture		get	
further		getting	
furthermore		ghost	
future		gift	
gain		girl	
gained		give	
gallant		gives	
gallon		given	
game		giving	
gang		glad	
garage		gladly	
garden		glance	
gas		glass	
gasoline		gloves	
gather		go	
gauge		goal	
gave		goes	
gems		going	
general		gold	
generally		golf	
generosity		gone	
generous		good	
gentle		goods	

good-will	*gdl*	gravity	*gvr*
got	*gt*	gray	*ga*
gotten	*gtn*	grease	*ge*
govern	*gvn*	great	*ga*
governed	*gvn*	greater	*gar*
governing	*gvng*	greatest	*gas*
government	*gvt*	greatly	*gal*
governmental	*gvt*	green	*ge*
governor	*gvnr*	greeting	*geg*
grace	*ga*	greetings	*geg*
gracious	*gy*	gritty	*gr*
grade	*ga*	grocery	*gsy*
graduate	*gda*	gross	*go*
graduated	*gda*	ground	*g*
graduating	*gdag*	group	*gu*
graduation	*gdj*	groves	*gv*
grain	*ga*	grow	*go*
grand	*g*	growing	*gog*
grant	*g*	grown	*gon*
granted	*g*	growth	*go*
grass	*gs*	guarantee	*g e*
grateful	*gay*	guaranteed	*g e*
gratifying	*glfg*	guaranty	*g e*
gratitude	*glu*	guard	*g*
grave	*gv*	guess	*gs*

114

Word	Shorthand	Word	Shorthand
guests		harder	
guidance		hardest	
guide		hardship	
guilty		hardware	
gums		has	
gun		have	
guy		having	
habits		hazards	
had		he	
hail		head	
half		headed	
hall		heading	
hand		headquarters	
handbook		health	
handle		healthy	
handled		hear	
handling		heard	
handsome		hearing	
handy		heart	
hang		heat	
happen		heater	
happened		heating	
happiness		heavier	
happy		heavy	
hard		heels	

height	_hi_	himself	_msf_
held	_hd_	hire	_hi_
help	_hp_	hired	_hi_
helped	_hp‾_	hiring	_hig‾_
helpful	_hpf_	his	_z_
helping	_hpg_	historical	_hskl_
hence	_h,_	history	_hsy_
her	_r_	hit	_hi_
here	_he_	hold	_hd_
hereafter	_heaf_	holding	_hdg_
herein	_hen_	holes	_ho_
hereto	_hel_	holiday	_hld_
herewith	_hew_	home	_ho_
hesitate	_hzta_	homeless	_hols_
hesitation	_hzty_	homes	_ho_
hidden	_hdn_	honest	_ons_
high	_hi_	honestly	_onsl_
higher	_hur_	honey	_hne_
highest	_his_	honorable	_onrb_
highlight	_hili_	honorary	_onry_
highly	_hil_	honored	_onr_
highway	_huwa_	hope	_ho‾_
hike	_hi_	hoped	_ho_
hills	_hl_	hopeful	_hof‾_
him	_m_	hoping	_hog_

horses	*hs*	icy	*ic*
hose	*hz*	idea	*ida*
hosiery	*hzy*	ideal	*ide*
hospital	*hspll*	identification	*id fkj*
hospitality	*hsplly*	identified	*id fi*
hospitalization	*hspllzy*	identify	*id fi*
host	*hs*	identity	*id*
hot	*hl*	if	*e*
hotel	*hll*	ill	*il*
hour	*r*	illness	*ilns*
hours	*r*	illustrated	*ilsa*
house	*hws*	illustrates	*ilsa*
housecleaning	*hwskeg*	illustration	*ilsj*
household	*hwshd*	illustrative	*ilsv*
housing	*hwzg*	imagine	*mgn*
how	*hw*	immediate	*imd*
however	*hwev*	immediately	*imd*
huge	*hj*	immune	*imu*
human	*hmn*	impact	*mpk*
hungry	*hgy*	impartial	*mpsl*
hunting	*h g*	impeller	*mplr*
hurry	*hy*	imperative	*mpv*
hurt	*h*	importance	*mp*
I	*I*	important	*mp*
ice	*is*	imported	*mp*

117

impose	*mpz*	inconvenienced	*nkvny*
imposed	*mpz*	incorporate	*ncrp*
impossible	*mpsB*	incorporated	*ncrp*
impressed	*mps*	incorporation	*ncrp*
impression	*mpsy*	incorrect	*nkrk*
imprint	*mp*	increase	*nke*
imprinted	*mp*	increased	*nke*
improved	*mpv*	increasing	*nkeg*
improvement	*mpv*	increasingly	*nkegl*
improving	*mpvg*	incur	*nkl*
in	*n*	incurred	*nkr*
inability	*nB*	indebtedness	*ndtns*
inadequate	*nagd*	indeed	*nde*
inasmuch	*nzmc*	indefinite	*ndfnl*
incentive	*hsnv*	indefinitely	*ndfnll*
inch	*nc*	indemnity	*ndmny*
incident	*nsd*	independence	*ndp*
incidentally	*nsd ll*	independent	*ndp*
inclined	*nkc*	index	*ndx*
include	*nku*	indexed	*ndx*
included	*nku*	indicate	*ndka*
including	*nkug*	indicated	*ndka*
inclusive	*nksv*	indicating	*ndkag*
income	*nk*	indication	*ndkf*
inconvenience	*nkvny*	indications	*ndky*

indirectly	*ndrkl*	inquiring	*nquq*
individual	*ndv*	inquiry	*nqy*
individually	*ndv*	insert	*ns*
industrial	*ndSl*	inserted	*ns*
industries	*ndSy*	inserting	*ns-q*
industry	*ndSy*	inside	*nsu*
inexpensive	*nxpn*	insist	*nsd*
inexperienced	*nxpz*	insofar	*nofr*
inflation	*nfy*	inspect	*nspk*
inflationary	*nfyy*	inspection	*nspky*
influence	*nfl*	inspector	*nspkr*
inform	*nfo*	inspiration	*nspry*
information	*nfo*	install	*nSl*
informative	*nfo*	installation	*nSly*
informed	*nfo*	installed	*nSl*
informing	*nfo*	installment	*nSl*
ingredients	*ngd*	instance	*nsy*
initial	*nzl*	instantly	*nsl*
initiation	*nzy*	instead	*nsd*
initiative	*nzv*	institute	*nStu*
injured	*nyr*	institution	*nSly*
injury	*nyy*	instruct	*nSk*
ink	*iq*	instructed	*nSk*
inked	*iq*	instruction	*nSky*
inquired	*nqu*	instructor	*nSkr*

119

instruments	*(shorthand)*	interruption	*(shorthand)*
insurance	*(shorthand)*	intersect	*(shorthand)*
insure	*(shorthand)*	interstate	*(shorthand)*
insured	*(shorthand)*	interval	*(shorthand)*
intact	*(shorthand)*	interview	*(shorthand)*
integral	*(shorthand)*	interworking	*(shorthand)*
intelligent	*(shorthand)*	into	*(shorthand)*
intend	*(shorthand)*	intrastate	*(shorthand)*
intended	*(shorthand)*	introduce	*(shorthand)*
intensive	*(shorthand)*	introduced	*(shorthand)*
intent	*(shorthand)*	introducing	*(shorthand)*
intention	*(shorthand)*	introduction	*(shorthand)*
interest	*(shorthand)*	introductory	*(shorthand)*
interested	*(shorthand)*	invent	*(shorthand)*
interesting	*(shorthand)*	inventories	*(shorthand)*
interim	*(shorthand)*	inventory	*(shorthand)*
interior	*(shorthand)*	invest	*(shorthand)*
interject	*(shorthand)*	invested	*(shorthand)*
interlapse	*(shorthand)*	investigating	*(shorthand)*
intermediate	*(shorthand)*	investigation	*(shorthand)*
intermit	*(shorthand)*	investment	*(shorthand)*
intermix	*(shorthand)*	investors	*(shorthand)*
internal	*(shorthand)*	invitation	*(shorthand)*
international	*(shorthand)*	invite	*(shorthand)*
interpretation	*(shorthand)*	invited	*(shorthand)*

invoice	*nvys*	journal	*jnl*
invoiced	*nvys*	judge	*jj*
involve	*nvv*	judgment	*jj*
involved	*nvv*	judiciary	*jdzy*
iron	*in*	juice	*ju*
irritating	*irlag*	June	*Jn*
is	*i*	junior	*jnr*
issue	*izu*	jurisdiction	*jsdky*
issued	*izu*	just	*js*
issuing	*izug*	keep	*ke*
it	*i*	keeping	*keg*
item	*itm*	kept	*kp*
items	*itm*	key	*ke*
itemized	*itmz*	keyboard	*keb*
itself	*isf*	kid	*kd*
jewelers	*jlr*	killed	*kl*
job	*jb*	killing	*klg*
jobber	*jbr*	kilowatts	*klwt*
jobs	*jb*	kind	*k*
join	*jyn*	kindest	*k S*
joined	*jyn*	kindly	*k l*
joining	*jyng*	kindnesses	*k ns*
joint	*jy*	kit	*kt*
jointly	*jy l*	kitchen	*kcn*
jot	*jt*	knack	*nk*

121

knew	*nu*	lasting	*lsg*
knife	*ni*	late	*la*
know	*n*	later	*lar*
knowing	*ng*	latest	*las*
knowledge	*nlj*	latex	*llx*
known	*no*	latter	*llr*
knows	*n*	launched	*lnc*
label	*lbl*	laundry	*ly*
labor	*lbr*	law	*la*
laboratory	*lbrly*	lawful	*laf*
lack	*lk*	lawn	*ln*
lading	*lag*	lawyer	*lyr*
lady	*ld*	lawyers	*lyr*
laid	*la*	lay	*la*
lake	*la*	layoff	*laof*
laminated	*lmna*	layout	*lao*
lamp	*lm*	lead	*le*
land	*l*	leader	*ler*
lane	*la*	leadership	*lerzp*
language	*lgj*	leading	*leg*
lapse	*lp*	leaf	*le*
large	*lj*	leaflet	*lell*
largely	*ljl*	league	*le*
largest	*ljs*	learn	*ln*
last	*ls*	learned	*ln*

122

learning	*lng*	level	*lvl*
lease	*le*	levied	*lv*
least	*ls*	liability	*lB*
leather	*l*	liable	*lB*
leave	*lv*	liberal	*lbl*
leaving	*lvg*	liberty	*lbt*
lecture	*lkcu*	librarians	*lbrn*
ledger	*lgr*	library	*lby*
left	*lf*	license	*lsn*
leg	*lg*	licensed	*lsn*
legal	*lgl*	lien	*le*
legislation	*lgsly*	lies	*le*
legislative	*lgslv*	lieu	*lu*
legislature	*lgslcu*	lieutenant	*lln*
lend	*l*	life	*le*
lender	*l*	lifetime	*lele*
length	*lg*	light	*le*
less	*ls*	lighting	*leg*
lesser	*lsr*	like	*le*
lesson	*lsn*	likely	*lel*
lessons	*lsn*	likewise	*lewz*
let	*le*	limit	*lml*
letter	*llr*	limitation	*lmly*
letterhead	*llrhd*	limited	*lml*
letting	*llg*	line	*le*

lines	*le*	locating	*lkag*
lining	*leg*	location	*lky*
liquid	*lgd*	lock	*lk*
liquidation	*lgdj*	logical	*gkl*
list	*lls*	long	*lg*
listed	*ls*	longer	*lgr*
listing	*lsg*	look	*lk*
literally	*lll*	looked	*lk*
literature	*llcr*	looking	*lkg*
little	*lll*	loop	*lu*
live	*lv*	loose	*lu*
lived	*lv*	lose	*lz*
livestock	*lvsk*	losing	*lzg*
living	*lvg*	loss	*ls*
load	*lo*	lost	*ls*
loaded	*lo*	lot	*ll*
loading	*log*	lotion	*ly*
loaf	*lo*	loud	*lud*
loan	*lo*	love	*lv*
loaned	*lo*	lovely	*lvl*
local	*lkl*	low	*lo*
localities	*lkl*	lower	*lor*
locality	*lkl*	lowest	*los*
locate	*lka*	loyal	*lyl*
located	*lka*	loyalty	*lyll*

124

lubrication	*lbky*	maker	*mar*
luck	*lk*	making	*mag*
lumber	*lmbr*	man	*mn*
lunch	*lnc*	management	*mmy*
luncheon	*lncn*	manager	*mnjr*
luxury	*lyy*	managing	*mnjg*
machine	*mje*	manila	*mnla*
machinery	*mjey*	mankind	*mnk*
madam	*mdm*	manner	*mnr*
made	*ma*	manual	*mnl*
magazine	*mgge*	manufacture	*mf*
magic	*mjk*	manufactured	*mf*
magnificent	*mgnfs*	manufacturer	*mf*
mahogany	*mhgne*	manufacturing	*mf*
mail	*ma*	manuscript	*mnskp*
mailed	*ma*	many	*m*
mailing	*mag*	map	*mp*
main	*ma*	margarine	*mjn*
maintain	*mala*	margin	*mjn*
maintained	*mala*	marine	*mre*
maintaining	*malag*	mark	*m*
maintenance	*maln*	marked	*m*
major	*mjr*	market	*m*
majority	*mjrs*	marketing	*m tg*
make	*ma*	marking	*m g*

marriage	*my*	measure	*mzr*
married	*my*	meat	*me*
marvel	*mrvl*	mechanical	*mknkl*
mass	*ms*	medical	*mdkl*
master	*msr*	medicine	*mdsn*
mat	*ml*	medium	*mdm*
match	*mc*	meet	*me*
material	*mlrl*	meetings	*meg*
materially	*mlrll*	meets	*me*
maternity	*mlrn*	member	*mmbr*
mathematics	*m—mlk*	membership	*mmbrzp*
matter	*mlr*	memo	*mmo*
mattress	*mls*	memorandum	*mmor—m*
maturity	*mcuz*	memorial	*mmrl*
maximum	*mxmm*	memory	*mmy*
may	*ma*	men	*mn*
maybe	*mab*	mention	*mnj*
mayor	*mr*	mentioned	*mnj*
maze	*mz*	merchandise	*mds*
me	*e*	merchandising	*mds*
meal	*me*	merchant	*mc*
mean	*me*	mercy	*mc*
meaning	*meg*	merely	*mel*
meantime	*melc*	merit	*mrl*
meanwhile	*mewc*	mesh	*mz*

126

message	*msj*	minority	*mnrly*
met	*ml*	minus	*mns*
metal	*mll*	minute	*mnl*
meter	*mlr*	mirror	*mrr*
method	*m-d*	miscellaneous	*mslny*
microphone	*mkfo*	misery	*myy.*
middle	*mdl*	mishap	*mhp*
might	*mi*	mishandle	*mhl*
mild	*md*	misjudge	*mjj*
mile	*mi*	misplaced	*mpa*
mileage	*my*	misprint	*mp*
miles	*mi*	miss	*ms*
military	*mlly*	missing	*msg*
milk	*mk*	mission	*mj*
mill	*ml*	mistake	*mla*
million	*mln*	mistaken	*mlan*
mimeographed	*mmgf*	misunderstanding	*musg*
mind	*m*	mixed	*mx*
minded	*m—*	mobilization	*mbz*
mineral	*mnl.*	model	*mdl*
miniature	*mncr*	modern	*mdn*
minimum	*mnmn*	modernization	*mdnz*
mining	*mng*	modest	*mdl*
minister	*mnsr*	moisture	*myscr*
minor	*mnr*	moment	*m*

money	*mne*	multiple	*mlpl*
month	*m*	multiply	*mlpi*
monthly	*ml*	municipal	*mnspl*
moral	*ml*	music	*mzk*
more	*mo*	musical	*mzkl*
morning	*mng*	must	*ms*
mortal	*ml*	mutual	*mcl*
mortgage	*mgy*	my	*m*
mortgagee	*mgje*	myself	*msf*
mortgagor	*mgyr*	name	*na*
most	*ms*	named	*na*
mostly	*msl*	namely	*nal*
motel	*mll*	nation	*ny*
mother	*m r*	national	*nyl*
motion	*my*	nationally	*nyll*
motor	*mlr*	native	*nv*
mounting	*m g*	natural	*ncl*
mouth	*mu*	naturally	*ncll*
move	*mv*	nature	*ncr*
moved	*mv*	near	*ne*
movement	*mv*	nearby	*neb*
movie	*mv*	nearest	*nes*
moving	*mvg*	nearly	*nel*
mower	*mbr*	neat	*ne*
much	*mc*	necessary	*nssy*

necessity	*nssy*	nicely	*nul*
need	*ne*	niece	*ne*
needed	*ne*	night	*nu*
needing	*neg*	no	*n*
needless	*nels*	noiseless	*nyfs*
needlessly	*nelsl*	nominal	*nmnl*
needs	*ne*	nominate	*nmna*
neglect	*ngk*	nominating	*nmnag*
neglected	*ngk*	nominees	*nmne*
neighbor	*nbr*	none	*n*
neighborhood	*nbrhd*	noon	*nu*
neighboring	*nbrg*	nor	*n*
neither	*n*	normal	*nml*
neon	*nn*	normally	*nmll*
nest	*ns*	north	*n*
net	*nl*	northern	*nn*
network	*nlw*	northwest	*nW*
never	*nv*	not	*n*
new	*nu*	notation	*nly*
newly	*nul*	note	*no*
news	*nz*	noted	*no*
newsletter	*nzltr*	notes	*no*
newspaper	*nzppr*	nothing	*ng*
next	*ny*	notice	*nls*
nice	*nu*	noticed	*nls*

notification	_nlfky_	obvious	_obvux_
notified	_nlfe_	obviously	_obvxl_
notify	_nlfe_	occasion	_oky_
notion	_ny_	occasionally	_okjll_
now	_nw_	occupation	_okpy_
number	_nmbr_	occupational	_okpjl_
numbered	_nmbr_	occur	_okr_
numbering	_nmbrg_	occurred	_okr_
numerous	_nms_	occurrence	_okr,_
nurse	_ns_	o'clock	_okk_
nursing	_nsg_	of	_v_
nylon	_nln_	off	_of_
oak	_ok_	offer	_ofr_
oath	_o_	offered	_ofr_
oats	_ol_	offering	_ofrg_
object	_objk_	office	_ofs_
objective	_objkv_	officer	_ofsr_
obligation	_obgy_	offices	_ofs_
oblige	_obj_	official	_ofx_
obliged	_obj_	officially	_ofxl_
observe	_obzv_	often	_of_
observed	_obzv_	oil	_yl_
obtain	_obla_	old	_od_
obtained	_obla_	older	_odr_
obtaining	_oblag_	oldest	_ods_

130

omitted	*oml*	ordinary	*ory*
on	*o*	organization	*og*
once	*urj*	organize	*og*
one	*urn*	organized	*og*
ones	*urn*	origin	*ojn*
only	*onl*	original	*orjnl*
open	*opn*	originally	*orjnll*
opened	*opn*	originating	*ojnag*
opening	*opng*	orphan	*ofn*
operate	*opra*	other	*or*
operated	*opra*	others	*or*
operating	*oprag*	otherwise	*o ruz*
operator	*oprar*	ought	*ol*
opinion	*opnn*	ounce	*urj*
opportunity	*op*	our	*r*
opposite	*opsl*	ourselves	*rsv*
optimistic	*oplmSk*	out	*O*
option	*opy*	outcome	*Ok*
optional	*opyl*	outdoor	*Odo*
or	*o*	outlets	*Oll*
orange	*orny*	outline	*Oli*
orchestra	*okSa*	outlined	*Oli*
order	*or*	outlining	*Olig*
ordered	*or*	outlook	*Olk*
ordering	*org*	output	*Opl*

131

outside	*Osu*	pair	*pa*
outstanding	*OS g*	pamphlet	*pmfl*
over	*V*	pan	*pn*
overage	*Vg*	panel	*pnl*
overall	*Vl*	paneling	*pnlg*
overhead	*Vhd*	paper	*ppr*
owe	*o*	paragraph	*prgf*
own	*on*	parcel	*psl*
owned	*on*	pardon	*p n*
owner	*onr*	parents	*p*
ownership	*onrзp*	parity	*pч*
package	*pkg*	park	*p*
packaged	*pkg*	parking	*p g*
packages	*pkg*	part	*p*
packaging	*pkgg*	partial	*pч*
packed	*pk*	participate	*plspa*
packets	*pkl*	participating	*plspag*
packing	*pkg*	participation	*plspj*
pad	*pd*	particular	*prl*
page	*py*	particularly	*prl*
paid	*pa*	particulars	*prl*
paid-up	*pa p*	partner	*p nr*
paint	*p*	parts	*p*
painted	*p*	part-time	*p lu*
painting	*p g*	party	*p l*

132

pass	*ps*	peak	*pe*
passage	*psy*	pecan	*pkn*
passed	*ps*	pen	*pn*
passenger	*psnyr*	penalty	*pnll*
passing	*psg*	pencil	*pnsl*
past	*ps*	pencils	*pnsl*
paste	*ps*	pending	*pg*
pastor	*psr*	penny	*pne*
pasture	*pscr*	pension	*pny*
patent	*pl*	people	*ppl*
patience	*pzs*	pepper	*ppr*
patient	*pz*	percent	*ps*
patio	*plo*	percentage	*psj*
patriotic	*pllk*	perfect	*pfk*
patrons	*pln*	perfectly	*pfkl*
pattern	*pln*	perform	*pfm*
pavilion	*pvln*	performance	*pfmy*
pay	*pa*	performed	*pfm*
payable	*paB*	perhaps	*phy*
payee	*pae*	period	*prd*
paying	*pag*	perish	*pz*
payment	*pa*	permanent	*pmn*
payroll	*paro*	permissible	*pmsB*
peace	*pe*	permission	*pmy*
peacetime	*pel*	permit	*pml*

permitted	*pml*	picked	*pk*
persistent	*psl*	picking	*pkg*
person	*psn*	pickup	*pkp*
personal	*psnl*	picture	*pkcr*
personality	*psnl*	pictures	*pkcr*
personalized	*psnl*	pie	*pi*
personally	*psnl*	piece	*pe*
personnel	*psnl*	pieces	*pe*
pertaining	*plag*	pin	*pn*
pertains	*pla*	pine	*pi*
pertinent	*p n*	pink	*pg*
pet	*pl*	pipe	*pi*
petition	*ply*	pity	*ps*
petroleum	*pllm*	place	*pa*
pharmacy	*fmc*	placed	*pa*
phase	*fz*	placement	*pa*
phone	*fo*	places	*pa*
phosphate	*fsfa*	plain	*pa*
phosphorous	*fsfs*	plan	*pn*
photo	*flo*	plane	*pa*
photograph	*flogf*	planned	*pn*
physical	*fzll*	planning	*png*
physician	*fzy*	plant	*p*
piano	*pno*	planted	*p*
pick	*pk*	plastic	*psk*

plate	*pa*	pool	*pu*
play	*pa*	poor	*pr*
played	*pa*	pop	*pp*
playing	*pag*	poppy	*pp*
pleasant	*pz*	popular	*pplr*
please	*pz*	popularity	*pplz*
pleased	*pz*	population	*pplz*
pleasing	*pzg*	portable	*p b*
pleasure	*pzu*	portfolio	*p flo*
pledge	*py*	portion	*py*
pledging	*pyg*	port	*p*
plentiful	*pf*	position	*pzz*
plenty	*pe*	positive	*pzv*
plow	*pw*	possession	*pzz*
plus	*ps*	possibility	*psbz*
pocket	*pkl*	possible	*psb*
point	*py*	possibly	*psbl*
pointed	*py*	post	*ps*
pole	*po*	postage	*psy*
policy	*plc*	postal	*psl*
policyholder	*plchdr*	posted	*ps*
polio	*plo*	poster	*psr*
polish	*plz*	posting	*psg*
political	*pllkl*	postmaster	*psmsr*
politics	*pllk*	potential	*plnt*

135

poultry		prepayment	
pound		presence	
power		present	
powered		presents	
powerful		presentation	
practicable		presented	
practical		presently	
practically		preserve	
practice		preserving	
praise		president	
precedence		presidential	
preceding		press	
precinct		pressed	
precision		pressure	
prefer		presumably	
preference		presume	
preferred		pretend	
preliminary		pretty	
premises		prevent	
premium		prevention	
preparation		preview	
preparatory		previous	
prepare		previously	
prepared		price	
preparing		priced	

pricer	*pur*
pricing	*pug*
pride	*pu*
primarily	*pmrl*
primary	*pmy*
prime	*pu*
principal	*pnspl*
principle	*pnspl*
print	*p*
printed	*p*
printer	*p r*
printing	*p g*
prior	*pr*
priority	*pry*
privacy	*pvc*
private	*pvt*
privilege	*pvlg*
prize	*pz*
probability	*pbBy*
probable	*pbB*
probably	*pbBl*
problem	*pbm*
problems	*pbm*
procedure	*psyr*
proceed	*pse*

proceedings	*pseg*
process	*pss*
processed	*pss*
processing	*pssg*
procure	*pku*
procurement	*pku*
produce	*pdu*
produced	*pdu*
producer	*pdur*
producing	*pdug*
product	*pdk*
production	*pdkj*
productivity	*pdkvy*
products	*pdk*
profession	*pfj*
professional	*pfjl*
professor	*pfsr*
profit	*pfl*
profitable	*pflB*
program	*pgm*
programmed	*pgm*
progress	*pgs*
project	*pjk*
prominent	*pmn*
promised	*pms*

promise	*pms*	protected	*plk*
promising	*pmsg*	protecting	*plkg*
promote	*pmo*	protection	*plkj*
promoted	*pmo*	protective	*plkv*
promoting	*pmog*	protest	*pls*
promotion	*pmj*	proud	*pwd*
promotional	*pmjl*	prove	*pv*
prompt	*pmp*	proved	*pv*
promptly	*pmpl*	proven	*pvn*
proof	*pu*	provide	*pvi*
proper	*ppr*	provided	*pvi*
properly	*pprl*	providing	*pvig*
property	*ppl*	proving	*pvg*
proportion	*ppj*	provision	*pvj*
proportionally	*ppjll*	proxy	*pxe*
proposal	*ppzl*	public	*pblk*
propose	*ppz*	publication	*pblkj*
proposed	*ppz*	publicity	*pbls*
proposition	*ppzj*	publish	*pblz*
prorate	*pra*	published	*pblz*
prospect	*pspk*	publisher	*pblzr*
prospective	*pspkv*	publishing	*pblzg*
prospectus	*pspks*	pullman	*plmn*
prosperous	*psps*	pumps	*pm*
protect	*plk*	punched	*pnc*

138

punches	*pnc*	quick	*qk*
punching	*pncg*	quicker	*qkr*
pupils	*ppl*	quickly	*qkl*
purchase	*pcs*	quiet	*ql*
purchased	*pcs*	quit	*ql*
purchaser	*pcsr*	quite	*qe*
purchasing	*pcsg*	quiver	*qvr*
pure	*pu*	quota	*qla*
purpose	*pps*	quotation	*qly*
purse	*ps*	quote	*qo*
pursuant	*ps*	quoted	*qo*
pursuit	*psu*	quoting	*qog*
push	*pz*	race	*rd*
put	*pl*	rack	*rk*
putting	*plg*	radio	*rdo*
qualifications	*qlfky*	rail	*ra*
qualified	*qlfe*	railroad	*raro*
qualify	*qlfe*	railway	*rawa*
quality	*qly*	rains	*ra*
quantity	*q*	raise	*rz*
quarrel	*qrl*	raised	*rz*
quart	*q*	ran	*rn*
quarter	*qr*	ranch	*rnc*
quarterly	*qrl*	range	*rny*
question	*qsy*	rangers	*rnyr*

ranging		realty	
rapid		ream	
rapidly		reason	
rare		reasonable	
rate		reasonably	
rated		recall	
rather		receipt	
rating		receivable	
rationing		receive	
raw		received	
reach		receiver	
reached		receiving	
reaching		recent	
reaction		recently	
read		reception	
reader		recess	
readily		recipient	
reading		recognition	
readjustment		recognize	
ready		recognized	
real		recognizes	
realize		recommend	
realized		recommendation	
realizing		recommended	
really		recommending	

140

record		refund	
recorded		refunded	
recorder		refuse	
recording		refused	
recover		regard	
recovery		regarding	
recreation		regardless	
recreational		regency	
red		region	
redemption		regional	
reduce		register	
reduced		registered	
reducing		registrant	
reduction		registrar	
refer		registration	
reference		registry	
references		regret	
referendum		regretting	
referred		regular	
referring		regularly	
refills		regulation	
refine		rehabilitation	
refinery		reinstated	
reflect		reinsurance	
refrigerated		related	

relating		reminder	
relations		remit	
relationship		remittance	
relative		remitted	
relatively		removal	
relax		remove	
relaxed		removed	
release		removes	
released		removing	
reliable		render	
reliance		rendered	
relief		renew	
religion		renewal	
religious		renewed	
reluctant		rent	
rely		rental	
remain		reorder	
remained		repaid	
remainder		repair	
remaining		repaired	
remarkable		repay	
remarks		repayment	
remember		repeat	
remembered		replace	
remind		replaced	

replacement	*(shorthand)*	resale	*(shorthand)*
replacing	*(shorthand)*	rescue	*(shorthand)*
reply	*(shorthand)*	research	*(shorthand)*
replying	*(shorthand)*	reservation	*(shorthand)*
report	*(shorthand)*	reserve	*(shorthand)*
reported	*(shorthand)*	reserved	*(shorthand)*
reporting	*(shorthand)*	resident	*(shorthand)*
represent	*(shorthand)*	resignation	*(shorthand)*
representation	*(shorthand)*	resist	*(shorthand)*
representative	*(shorthand)*	resolution	*(shorthand)*
represented	*(shorthand)*	resolve	*(shorthand)*
representing	*(shorthand)*	resolved	*(shorthand)*
reprint	*(shorthand)*	resources	*(shorthand)*
reprinted	*(shorthand)*	respect	*(shorthand)*
reproduced	*(shorthand)*	respected	*(shorthand)*
reproduction	*(shorthand)*	respectfully	*(shorthand)*
reputation	*(shorthand)*	respective	*(shorthand)*
request	*(shorthand)*	respectively	*(shorthand)*
requested	*(shorthand)*	respond	*(shorthand)*
requesting	*(shorthand)*	response	*(shorthand)*
require	*(shorthand)*	responsibility	*(shorthand)*
required	*(shorthand)*	responsible	*(shorthand)*
requirement	*(shorthand)*	rest	*(shorthand)*
requiring	*(shorthand)*	restraint	*(shorthand)*
requisition	*(shorthand)*	restricted	*(shorthand)*

restriction	*rSky*	reward	*rw*
result	*rzl*	ribbon	*rbn*
resulted	*rzl*	rich	*rc*
resulting	*rzlg*	ride	*ru*
resume	*rzu*	rider	*rur*
retail	*rla*	riding	*rug*
retailer	*rlar*	right	*ru*
retain	*rla*	ring	*rg*
retained	*rla*	ringing	*rgg*
retire	*rli*	rise	*rz*
retirement	*rli*	rising	*rzg*
return	*rln*	risk	*rs*
returnable	*rlnB*	road	*ro*
returned	*rln*	roads	*ro*
returning	*rlng*	roast	*rS*
revenue	*rvnu*	robe	*ro*
reverse	*rvs*	rods	*rd*
review	*rvu*	role	*ro*
reviewed	*rvu*	roll	*ro*
reviewing	*rvug*	rolling	*rog*
revise	*rvz*	roof	*ru*
revised	*rbz*	roofing	*rug*
revision	*rvj*	room	*ru*
revolutionary	*rvlyy*	rope	*ro*
revolving	*rvvg*	rose	*rz*

roster	*rSr*	salesman	*samn*
rough	*rf*	salt	*sl*
round	*r*	salvage	*svj*
route	*ru*	same	*sa*
routing	*rug*	sample	*smpl*
rows	*ro*	samples	*smpl*
rubber	*rbr*	sand	*s*
rude	*ru*	sanitary	*snly*
rug	*rg*	sat	*sl*
rule	*ru*	satisfaction	*sl*
run	*rn*	satisfactorily	*sl*
running	*rng*	satisfactory	*sl*
rural	*rl*	satisfied	*sl*
rush	*rz*	satisfy	*sl*
sack	*sk*	save	*sv*
sacrifice	*skf*	saved	*sv*
sadly	*sdl*	saver	*svr*
safe	*sa*	saving	*svg*
safeguard	*sag*	saw	*s*
safety	*sfl*	say	*sa*
said	*sd*	saying	*sag*
sailings	*sag*	says	*sz*
salaried	*sly*	scale	*ska*
salary	*sly*	scenic	*sek*
sale	*sd*	scheduled	*skju*

145

schedule	*skju*	security	*skuz*
scheme	*ske*	see	*c*
scholarship	*sklrzp*	seed	*se*
school	*sku*	seeding	*seg*
science	*sy*	seeing	*c*
scope	*sko*	seek	*se*
score	*sko*	seeking	*seg*
scoring	*skog*	seem	*se*
scrap	*skp*	seemed	*se*
screen	*ske*	seen	*c*
screening	*skeg*	seldom	*sdm*
seal	*se*	select	*slk*
search	*sc*	selected	*slk*
season	*Czn*	selecting	*slkg*
seasonal	*Cznl*	selection	*slkj*
second	*sk*	selective	*slkv*
secret	*ckl*	self	*sf*
secretarial	*sklrl*	sell	*sl*
secretary	*skly*	seller	*slr*
section	*skj*	selling	*slg*
sectional	*skjl*	semester	*smsr*
sections	*skj*	semiannual	*smanl*
secure	*sku*	senate	*snl*
secured	*sku*	senator	*snlr*
securing	*skug*	send	*s*

sending		setup	
senior		several	
sensational		severe	
sense		sew	
sent		sewing	
sentence		shade	
separate		shall	
separately		shame	
serial		shape	
series		share	
serious		shareholders	
sermon		shares	
servant		sharing	
serve		sharp	
served		she	
service		sheet	
servicemen		shelf	
servicing		shells	
serving		shelter	
session		sheltered	
set		shift	
setting		ship	
settle		shipment	
settled		shipped	
settlement		shipper	

147

shipping		side	
shirt		sight	
shoe		sign	
shoes		signal	
shoot		signature	
shooting		signed	
shop		signers	
shopping		significance	
shops		significant	
short		silence	
shortage		silk	
shortcut		silver	
shortest		similar	
shorthand		simple	
shortly		simplified	
shot		simplify	
should		simply	
show		simultaneously	
showed		since	
showing		sincere	
shown		sincerely	
shrink		single	
shut		singular	
sick		sink	
sickness		sinking	

sir	*sr*	social	*sɥ*
sister	*ssr*	society	*ssɏ*
site	*su*	soft	*sf*
situation	*sul*	soil	*syl*
size	*sz*	sold	*sd*
sizes	*sz*	soldiers	*sdr*
sketch	*skc*	solicit	*slsl*
skill	*skl*	solid	*sld*
skin	*skn*	solution	*sly*
slack	*sk*	solve	*sv*
sleep	*se*	solved	*sv*
slide	*su*	some	*sm*
slight	*su*	someone	*smwon*
slightly	*sul*	something	*sm g*
slip	*sp*	sometime	*smle*
slow	*so*	somewhat	*smwl*
small	*sml*	somewhere	*smwa*
smaller	*smlr*	son	*sn*
smallest	*smlS*	songs	*sg*
smart	*sm*	soon	*su*
smile	*sme*	sooner	*sur*
smoke	*smo*	sorry	*sy*
smooth	*sm*	sort	*sl*
so	*o*	sought	*sl*
soap	*so*	sought-after	*sl af*

149

sound	_s_	speech	_spc_
source	_ss_	speed	_spe_
south	_S_	speeds	_spe_
southeast	_SE_	spend	_sp_
southeastern	_SEn_	spending	_sp g_
southern	_Sn_	spent	_sp_
southwest	_SW_	spirit	_spl_
southwestern	_SWn_	spiritual	_spcl_
space	_spa_	spite	_spi_
spaced	_spa_	splendid	_sp d_
spacious	_spu_	spoke	_spo_
spare	_spa_	sponsor	_spnsr_
speak	_spe_	sponsored	_spnsr_
speaker	_sper_	sponsoring	_spnsrg_
speakers	_sper_	spools	_spu_
speaking	_speg_	sport	_sp_
special	_spy_	spouse	_spws_
specialists	_spys_	spread	_spd_
specialized	_spyz_	spring	_spg_
specially	_spyl_	square	_Sqa_
specific	_spc_	stable	_Sb_
specifically	_spc_	stabilization	_Sbzy_
specification	_spc_	staff	_Sf_
specifications	_spc_	stage	_Sj_
specify	_spc_	stakes	_Sa_

stamped		steamed	
stamps		steel	
stand		stem	
standard		steno	
standing		stenographer	
staple		step	
star		stern	
start		stewardship	
started		still	
starting		stimulate	
state		stimulating	
stated		stitching	
statement		stock	
statewide		stockholders	
stating		stocking	
station		stone	
stationery		stop	
statistical		stopping	
statistics		storage	
status		store	
statutory		stored	
stay		storekeeper	
steadily		stores	
steady		storm	
steam		story	

straight	*Sa*	styles	*Su*
straighten	*San*	subcontractors	*sklkr*
strategy	*Slg*	subject	*sjk*
street	*Se*	sublime	*sli*
strength	*Sg*	submission	*smy*
strengthen	*Sgn*	submit	*sml*
stretch	*Sc*	submitted	*sml*
stricken	*Skn*	submerge	*smy*
strict	*Sk*	subscribe	*sski*
strictly	*Skl*	subscriber	*sskr*
strike	*Si*	subscribing	*sskig*
strive	*Sv*	subscription	*sskpy*
strong	*Sg*	subsequent	*ssq*
stronger	*Sgr*	subside	*ssi*
strongly	*Sgl*	subsistence	*ssl*
struck	*Sk*	substance	*sls*
structure	*Skcr*	substantial	*sSns*
struggle	*Sgl*	substantially	*sSnsl*
stub	*Sb*	substitute	*sStu*
student	*Sd*	substitution	*sSly*
students	*Sd*	succeed	*skse*
study	*Sd*	succeeded	*skse*
studying	*Sdg*	succeeding	*skseg*
style	*Si*	success	*skss*
styled	*Si*	successes	*skss*

152

successful		supervision	
successfully		supervisor	
such		supervisory	
sudden		supplement	
sufficient		supplemental	
sufficiently		supplementary	
sugar		supplemented	
suggest		supplied	
suggested		supply	
suggesting		supplying	
suggestion		support	
suit		supported	
suitable		supporting	
suited		suppose	
suits		supposed	
sum		sure	
summarizing		surely	
summary		surface	
summer		surgeons	
sun		surgery	
sunny		surgical	
superintendent		surplus	
superintendent's		surprise	
superior		surprising	
supervising		surrounding	

survey	_Sva_	tape	_la_
suspended	_ssp_	target	_tgt_
suspense	_ssp,_	tariff	_trf_
sustained	_ssa_	task	_ts_
swamps	_swm_	taste	_ts_
swimming	_swmg_	taught	_tt_
swing	_swg_	tax	_tx_
switch	_swc_	taxable	_txB_
syllable	_slB_	taxation	_txy_
symphony	_smfne_	taxed	_txt_
system	_ssm_	taxpayer	_txpar_
tab	_tb_	teach	_tc_
table	_tB_	teacher	_tcr_
tablet	_tbll_	teaches	_tc_
tabulated	_tbla_	teaching	_tcg_
tabulating	_tblag_	team	_te_
tack	_tk_	tear	_ta_
tags	_tg_	technical	_tknkl_
take	_ta_	technique	_tkne_
taken	_tan_	teeth	_t_
taking	_tag_	telephone	_tlfo_
talk	_tlk_	television	_tlvy_
talked	_tlk_	tell	_tl_
talking	_tlkg_	telling	_tlg_
tank	_tg_	temporarily	_tmprl_

temporary		them	
tennis		theme	
tentative		themselves	
term		then	
terminal		theory	
terminate		there	
terminated		thereafter	
termination		thereby	
termites		therefor	
terms		therefore	
terrible		therein	
territory		thereof	
test		thereon	
tested		thereto	
text		these	
textbook		they	
texts		thick	
than		thickness	
thank		thing	
thankful		think	
thanking		thinking	
that		this	
the		thorough	
theater		thoroughly	
their		those	

though		toil	
thought		told	
thousand		tomorrow	
threat		ton	
thrilled		too	
through		took	
throughout		tool	
throw		top	
thrown		topic	
thus		tornado	
ticket		totaled	
tie		total	
tied		totally	
tight		touch	
timber		tour	
time		tourist	
timely		toward	
timing		tower	
tire		town	
title		towns	
to		toy	
toast		trace	
toaster		track	
today		tractor	
together		trade	

156

traded	
trade-mark	
trading	
tradition	
traffic	
tragic	
trail	
train	
trained	
training	
transact	
transaction	
transcript	
transcription	
transfer	
transferred	
transform	
transfusion	
transit	
transmission	
transmit	
transparent	
transplant	
transport	
transportation	

trap	
travel	
traveling	
tray	
treasure	
treasurer	
treasury	
treat	
treated	
treating	
treatment	
treaty	
trees	
tremendous	
tremendously	
trend	
trial	
tried	
trim	
trip	
triplicate	
trouble	
truce	
truck	
trucking	

true	*lu*	unable	*uaß*
truly	*lul*	unanimously	*unnmsl*
trust	*18*	unbend	*ub*
trustees	*18e*	unchanged	*ucng*
trusting	*18g*	uncle	*al*
truth	*1L*	uncommon	*ukn*
try	*lu*	uncut	*ukl*
trying	*lug*	uneasy	*uez*
tube	*lu*	under	*U*
tuberculosis	*lbklss*	undergraduate	*Ugda*
tuition	*ly*	understand	*US*
tune	*lu*	understanding	*USg*
turn	*ln*	understood	*USd*
turnover	*lnp*	undertaken	*Ulan*
twice	*lwi*	undertaking	*Ulag*
twin	*lwn*	underwrite	*Uru*
twine	*lwi*	underwriting	*Urug*
type	*lu*	undivided	*udvi*
typed	*lu*	undoubtedly	*udwll*
types	*li*	unemployed	*umpy*
typewriter	*lurr*	unemployment	*umpy*
typewriting	*lurg*	unfair	*ufa*
typical	*lpkl*	unfed	*ufd*
typing	*lug*	unfilled	*ufl*
typist	*lus*	unfortunate	*ufcnl*

unfortunately		upholstered	
ungracious		upholstering	
unheard		upon	
uniform		upper	
union		upward	
unique		urge	
unit		urged	
united		urgent	
universal		urgently	
university		urging	
unless		us	
unloading		usage	
unmarried		use	
unnecessary		used	
unpaid		useful	
unprecedented		user	
unrest		using	
unsafe		usual	
unshipped		usually	
unsurpasses		utilities	
until		utility	
unto		utilize	
unused		utilized	
unusual		utmost	
up		vacation	

valuable	*vluB*	vigor	*vgr*
value	*vlu*	vigorously	*vgrsl*
valued	*vlu*	violations	*vlf*
values	*vlu*	virtually	*vrll*
van	*vn*	visible	*vzB*
varied	*vry*	vision	*vy*
variety	*vry*	visit	*vzt*
various	*vrx*	visited	*vzt*
varsity	*vsy*	visiting	*vztg*
vary	*vry*	visits	*bzt*
vast	*vs*	visual	*vx*
vegetable	*vjlB*	vital	*vll*
vehicle	*vkl*	vitally	*vlll*
vendor	*vr*	vocational	*vkjl*
ventilator	*v lar*	voice	*vys*
venture	*vncu*	volume	*vlm*
vertical	*v kl*	voluntary	*vl y*
very	*v*	vote	*vo*
veteran	*vln*	voted	*vo*
vice	*vr*	voters	*vor*
vicinity	*vsny*	voting	*vog*
victory	*vky*	voucher	*vwcr*
view	*vu*	vowel	*vwl*
viewer	*vur*	wage	*wj*
vigilance	*vjls*	wagon	*wgn*

wait		we	
waited		weakness	
waiting		wealth	
walk		wear	
wall		weather	
wallpaper		webbing	
walnut		wee	
want		week	
wanted		weekly	
war		weeks	
wardrobe		weighing	
warehouse		weight	
warehousemen		welcome	
warmer		welfare	
warrant		well	
warranty		went	
wartime		west	
was		western	
washing		what	
waste		whatever	
watch		wheat	
watches		wheel	
watchful		when	
water		whenever	
way		where	

whereas	*waz*	winning	*wng*
whereby	*wab*	winter	*wr*
wherever	*walv*	wipe	*wr*
whether	*wr*	wire	*wr*
which	*wc*	wired	*wr*
while	*wr*	wiring	*wrg*
white	*wr*	wise	*wz*
who	*w*	wish	*wz*
whole	*ho*	with	*w*
wholesale	*hosa*	withdraw	*w da*
wholesaler	*hosar*	withdrawals	*w dal*
whom	*w*	withdrawn	*w dan*
whose	*wz*	withheld	*w hd*
why	*y*	withholding	*w hdg*
wide	*wr*	within	*w n*
widely	*wrl*	without	*w d*
wider	*wr*	withstand	*w s*
width	*wd*	witness	*wtns*
wife	*wr*	witty	*w*
will	*l*	woman	*wmn*
willing	*lg*	women	*wmn*
win	*wn*	won	*wn*
wind	*w*	wonder	*wr*
window	*w o*	wonderful	*wr*
winner	*wnr*	wonderfully	*wr*

wondering		writing	
wood		written	
wool		wrong	
word		wrote	
wording		x-ray	
words-a-minute		yard	
work		year	
workable		years	
worked		yearly	
worker		yellow	
working		yes	
workmanship		yesterday	
workshop		yet	
world		yield	
worn		you	
worry		young	
worth		youngsters	
worthwhile		yours	
worthy		yourself	
would		youth	
wrap		zone	
wrapping			
wrinkles			
write			
writer			

STENOSCRIPT ABC SHORTHAND DICTIONARY

PART II

Vocational Dictionary — Additional Words Used Extensively In The Following Fields:

Aircraft

Construction

Contract

Legal

Medical

Missile

accelerated	*akslra*	comparable	*kpß*
accumulators	*agmllr*	comprehensive	*kphrv*
aerodynamics	*ardnmnk*	conducted	*kdk*
aileron	*alrn*	contractual	*Kku*
aircraft	*arkf*	controllability	*Klbr*
altering	*alrg*	cowling	*kwlg*
alternator	*alnlr*	defensive	*dfrv*
anti-icing	*an rsg*	deicing	*disg*
assembly	*asml*	descend	*ds*
atmospheric	*almsfrk*	diagonal	*dgnl*
authorization	*a rzy*	dihedral	*dhdrl*
aviation	*avy*	dorsal	*dsl*
axis	*avs*	drag	*dg*
bomb bay	*bm ba*	droppable	*dpß*
bombers	*bmr*	Duralumin	*dralmn*
bombing	*bmg*	echelon	*ezln*
budget	*byt*	extensive	*xlrv*
calculators	*kkllr*	fairing	*fag*
calibrate	*klba*	fin	*fn*
camber	*kmbr*	finalize	*fnlz*
certified	*sfr*	flaperon	*fprn*
centrifugal force	*s fgl fr*	flutter	*flr*
chord	*k*	formalize	*fmlz*
chute	*zu*	functional	*fyl*
communication	*kmnky*	fuselage	*fzlg*

167

hydraulic	*hdlk*	plexiglas	*pxgs*
increment	*nk*	potential	*plnx*
inflammable	*nfmB*	practicable	*pkB*
integrated	*nlga*	preservation	*pzvy*
intensive	*nly*	proficiency	*pfync*
internal	*Nnl*	propulsion	*ppy*
inverter	*nv*	radar	*rdr*
jawing	*pvg*	radome	*rdo*
jet	*jt*	ratio	*rzo*
jig	*jg*	reactive	*rakv*
lateral	*lll*	reconnaissance	*rks,*
leading edge	*leg ey*	regulation	*rgly*
liaison	*lyn*	replaceable	*rpaB*
longitudinal	*lngtdnl*	retractable landing gear	*rlkB ge g*
magnesium	*mgnym*	rotated	*rla*
mandatory	*m ly*	rudder	*rdr*
maneuverability	*mnvrlG*	salvage	*svy*
mufflers	*mflr*	sebac	*sbk*
nacelle	*nsl*	segregate	*sgrga*
nominal	*nmnl*	slat	*sl*
operable	*oprB*	slot	*sl*
pertinent	*p n*	span	*spn*
pickled	*pkl*	spar	*spr*
pitot tube	*pll lu*	stabilizer	*SGyr*
plastic	*pSk*		

168

stratofreighter	_(shorthand)_
stratojet	_(shorthand)_
stratoliner	_(shorthand)_
streamlining	_(shorthand)_
strut	_(shorthand)_
subsidies	_(shorthand)_
supremacy	_(shorthand)_
sweptback	_(shorthand)_
tapering	_(shorthand)_
targets	_(shorthand)_
thermal	_(shorthand)_
tolerance	_(shorthand)_
transportable	_(shorthand)_
unstable	_(shorthand)_
visibility	_(shorthand)_

abutment	*abt*	cathode	*k o*
acetylene	*aSln*	cellular	*sllr*
acoustic	*akSk*	centrifugal	*s fgl*
adhesion	*ahj*	ceramic	*smk*
admixture	*amyu*	clamshell	*kmzl*
agitator	*ajtar*	cofferdam	*kfrdm*
air-entrained	*arnla*	compaction	*kpkj*
airproof	*arpu*	conduit	*kdl*
amperage	*mpj*	conical	*kkl*
annealing	*aneg*	counterweight	*Kwa*
anode	*ano*	coupling	*kplg*
antifriction	*alfkj*	crankshaft	*kazf*
apron	*apn*	crawler	*kbl*
arc welding	*rk wdg*	creosoted	*kso*
asphaltic	*asflk*	crucible	*ksB*
bedrock	*bdrk*	cupola	*gpla*
backfilling	*bkflg*	curing	*qug*
bevel	*bvl*	cylindrical	*sl kl*
bulkhead	*bkhd*	dampproofing	*dppug*
bulldozer	*bldzr*	datum	*dtm*
buoyant	*by*	dehydration	*dhdj*
caisson	*ksn*	deoxidation	*doxdj*
calibration	*klbj*	derrick	*drk*
calking	*kkg*	detonation	*dtng*
cantilever	*k lvr*	dewater	*dwtr*

170

diesel	*dzl*	heliarc	*hlrk*
ditcher	*dcr*	holing-through	*hog—u*
dragline	*dgl*	hopper	*hpr*
drawbar	*dwbr*	hydrated	*hdra*
dry dock	*de dk*	hydraulic	*hdlk*
ductility	*dkl*	hydroelectric	*hdelklk*
earth-moving	*e mvg*	ingot	*ngt*
electrodes	*elkls*	inlets	*nll*
electrolytic	*elklk*	intake	*nla*
emulsified	*emsfe*	jackhammer	*jkhmr*
erosion	*erj*	joist	*jys*
ferrous	*frs*	jumbo	*jmbo*
foot-pound	*fl p*	kiln	*kn*
formwork	*fmw*	lagging	*lgg*
generator	*jnrar*	laminated	*lmna*
girder	*gr*	lathe	*l*
gneiss	*ni*	limestone	*liSo*
gooseneck	*gunk*	louver	*lvr*
gradation	*gdj*	macadam	*mkdm*
graphite	*gfe*	magnesium	*mgnym*
grout	*ga*	mandrel	*m l*
gypsum	*gpsm*	manganese	*mgnz*
hammerhead	*hmrhd*	masonry	*msny*
headframe	*hdra*	monolithic	*mnl k*
heavy-duty	*hvdl*	nonferrous	*nfrs*

outrigger	*Orgr*	spillover	*sply*
oxyacetylene	*xslln*	spillway	*splwa*
parabolic	*pblk*	stabilization	*Sbz*
penstock	*pnSk*	stiffleg	*Sflg*
permafrost	*pmfS*	stringer	*Sgr*
permeable	*pmb*	stud welding	*Sd wdg*
pilaster	*plSr*	subbase	*sba*
plumbness	*pmns*	subgrade	*sga*
plywood	*pwwd*	subsoil	*ssyl*
pneumatic	*nmlk*	subsurface	*ssfs*
portland cement	*pls*	sump	*sp*
precast	*pkS*	superhighway	*sprhwa*
prefabricated	*pfbka*	superstructure	*spSku*
prestress	*pSs*	suspension	*spny*
refractory	*rfky*	tandem	*lm*
resilience	*rsls*	tarpaulin	*lpln*
salamander	*sl r*	tempered	*lmpr*
sandblast	*s bS*	templates	*lmpa*
sandstone	*s So*	tensile	*lnsl*
scaffold	*skfd*	thermal	*ml*
scarifier	*skrfr*	tie bar	*le br*
sedimentation	*sdj*	torque	*lk*
silicon	*slkn*	tractor	*lkr*
siphon	*sfn*	transverse	*Tvs*
solder	*Sdr*	tremie	*lme*

172

trencher	_trncr_
turbine	_tbn_
underpinning	_Upng_
vibrator	_vbtr_
viscosity	_vsks,_
wallboards	_wlb_
water-resistant	_whrzs_
winch	_wnc_
windrow	_w~ro_

accord & satisfaction	*ak/ & sl*	condonation	*kdny*
actionable rights	*abß ru*	conspiracy	*kspri*
administrative law	*adm la*	contractual obligations	*Kk+ obgy*
administrators	*adm*	contractual rights	*Kk+ ru*
anticipatory breach	*alsply bc*	conversion	*kvy*
arson	*asn*	copyright	*kpri*
assault and battery	*asl & bly*	cross-examination	*ksymny*
assignment	*asu*	deliberate concealment	*dlbra ksl*
breach of contract	*bc Kk*	deliberate misrepresentation	*dlbra mrp*
bucket-shop transactions	*bkl zp Jaky*	divisible contract	*dvyß Kk*
cause of action	*ky v aky*	due process of law	*d pss v la (dpla)*
chancery courts	*cnay k*	embezzlement	*mbyl*
choses in action	*zo n aky*	enforceable at law	*nfsßl la*
commercial paper	*kmy ppr*	executed contract	*xku Kk*
common law	*kmn la*	executors	*xkur*
competitive bidders	*kplv bdr*	express contract	*xps Kk*
composition with creditors	*kpzy w kdlr*	executory contract	*xkly Kk*
compound interest	*kp nß*	express offer	*xps ofr*
compromise agreement	*kpmy age*	false statements	*fa Sa*
contempt of court	*klmp v k*		

Federal constitution	*fdl kSly*	interstate trade	*nSa la*
felonies	*flne*	intestate	*nlSa*
forgery	*fjy*	invalid consideration	*nvld ksdry*
formal contract	*fml Kk*	irrevocable	*irvkS*
formal documents	*fml dk*	judgment by default	*jj—b dfl*
fraudulent assignment	*fdl asi*	larceny	*lsne*
fraudulent statement	*fdl sa*	latent defects	*ll—dfk*
general release	*jnl rle*	law courts	*la k*
governing authority	*gvng ary*	law enforcement	*la nfs*
implied acceptance	*mpi—xps*	law of procedure	*la v psdu*
implied contract	*mpi Kk*	lawsuit	*lasu*
indenture	*nd u*	legal consideration	*lgl ksdry*
infringements	*nfnj*	legal detriment	*lgl dl*
innocent misrepresentative	*ns—mrp*	legal document	*lgl dk*
insolvent debtor	*nsv dlr*	legal form	*lgl fm*
intangible property	*nlnjS pps*	legal incapacity	*lgl nkpsi*
international law	*Nnjl la*	legal obligation	*lgl obgs*
interstate commerce	*nSa kms*	legal tender	*lgl lr*
		lobbying	*lbg*
		lucid moments	*lsd m*

marriage settlement	*my sll*	oral contracts	*ol Kk*
material alteration	*mlrl alry*	original claim	*ojnl ka*
material fact	*mlrl fk*	parol-evidence rule	*prl evds ru*
meeting of the minds	*meg v m*	police power	*pls pwr*
maximum legal rate	*mxmm lgl ra*	political preference	*pllkl pfp*
money damages	*mne dmy*	power of attorney	*pwr v alne*
moral law	*ml la*	principle of law	*prpl v la*
moral obligations	*ml obgs*	private law	*pvl la*
mutual agreement	*mcl age*	proof of claim	*pu v ka*
mutual assent	*mcl as*	property rights	*ppy ru*
mutual mistake	*mcl mla*	public law	*pbk la*
National Bankruptcy Act	*nyl bgrpc ak (NBA)*	public policy	*pbk plc*
natural incapacity	*ncl nkpcy*	qualified acceptance	*glfr xps*
nominal damages	*nmnl dmy*	reality of agreement	*rly v age*
noncompliance	*nkpy*	reasonable time	*rznB le*
nondisclosure	*ndkzu*	restraint of trade	*rS la*
novation	*nvy*	revocation	*rvky*
offeror	*ofrr*	right of action	*ru v aky*
operation of law	*opry la*	right of eminent domain	*ru v mn dma*
option	*opy*	several liability	*svl lBy*
		simple contract	*smpl Kk*

specialty contract	*spyl Kk*
specific goods	*spsfk gd*
specific performance	*spsfk pfm, *
state legislature	*Sa lgslcu*
statute law	*Slu la*
statute of frauds	*Slu v fd*
statutory provision	*Slly pvy*
stipulations	*Sply*
stock transactions	*Sk Faky*
subject matter	*sjk mlr*
subpoena	*Spna*
successive parties	*sksv p²*
surrogates courts	*sga k*
tangible property	*lnjB pp,*
tender of performance	*L r v pfm,*
testator	*lsar*
third party	*/ p²*
torts	*l*
trade-marks	*la m*
trade secrets	*la skl*

transfer of title	*Ifr v lll*
trespass	*lsps*
undisputed claim	*udpu ka*
undue influence	*ud nf,*
unenforceable promise	*unfsB pms*
unwritten law	*urln la*
usurious contracts	*usy Kk*
valid consideration	*vld ksdy*
voidable contract	*vydB Kk*
voluntary bankruptcy	*vl y bqrpk*
wagering contracts	*ujrg Kk*
written law	*rln la*

177

acceptance for honor	*xps f onr*	board of directors	*b drkr*
acceptance supra protest	*xps sprapls*	bona fide	*bna fe*
acceptor	*xpr*	breach of warranty	*bc v wr e*
accommodation note	*akdy no*	capital stock	*Apll Sk*
administrator	*adm*	cash surrender value	*kz s r vlu*
adverse possession	*ave pzz*	casualty insurance	*kyl nzuy*
agency by implication	*agnc b mpky*	caveat emptor	*kvl mplr*
alienation clause	*alny kz*	cease and desist order	*se a r dyS o s fka*
allonge	*alny*	certificate of deposit	*v dpzl fka*
articles of copartnership	*rlkl v kp nyp*	certificate of incorporation	*s fka v ncrp*
assignability	*asB*	certificate of registration	*s fka v rySy*
attorneys at law	*alne l la*	certification	*s fky*
auctioneers	*akje*	charter	*cr*
average clause policy	*avy kz plc*	close corporation	*kz crp*
bearer instrument	*bar nl*	coercion	*kry*
bequest	*bgS*	coguarantors	*kgr r*
bill of exchange	*bl v xcny*	coinsurance clause policy	*knzuy kz plc*
binding slip	*bg sp*	collaterial trust bonds	*kllc lS b*
blank indorsement	*bg nds*	collective bargaining	*klkv bgng*

178

common-law liability	*[shorthand]*	endowment policy	*[shorthand]*
conditional indorsement	*[shorthand]*	equity of redemption	*[shorthand]*
constructive notice	*[shorthand]*	escheat	*[shorthand]*
continuing guaranty	*[shorthand]*	estate in fee simple	*[shorthand]*
contract of suretyship	*[shorthand]*	estate in remainder	*[shorthand]*
cumulative voting	*[shorthand]*	estate in severalty	*[shorthand]*
days of grace	*[shorthand]*	estate of courtesy	*[shorthand]*
debenture bonds	*[shorthand]*	estate of inheritance	*[shorthand]*
decedent estate laws	*[shorthand]*	estoppel	*[shorthand]*
deed	*[shorthand]*	false pretenses	*[shorthand]*
defense clause	*[shorthand]*	Fair Labor Standards Act	*[shorthand]*
del credere agent	*[shorthand]*	fidelity insurance	*[shorthand]*
delivery in escrow	*[shorthand]*	Federal Revenue Act	*[shorthand]*
demand & notice waived	*[shorthand]*	fellow-servant rule	*[shorthand]*
devise	*[shorthand]*	financial responsibility laws	*[shorthand]*
dormant partner	*[shorthand]*	for value received	*[shorthand]*
dower	*[shorthand]*	foreign bill of exchange	*[shorthand]*
emblements	*[shorthand]*	forfeiture	*[shorthand]*
eminent domain	*[shorthand]*		

179

fraudulent concealment	*(shorthand)*	insufficient funds	*(shorthand)*
freehold estate	*(shorthand)*	insurable interest	*(shorthand)*
full warranty deed	*(shorthand)*	intestacy	*(shorthand)*
good will	*(shorthand)*	involuntary release	*(shorthand)*
gratuitous agent	*(shorthand)*	irregular indorser	*(shorthand)*
guaranty of collection	*(shorthand)*	irrevocable agency	*(shorthand)*
guaranty of payment	*(shorthand)*	joint and several notes	*(shorthand)*
holder in due course	*(shorthand)*	joint returns	*(shorthand)*
homestead estate	*(shorthand)*	joint tenancy	*(shorthand)*
hostile fires	*(shorthand)*	judgment note	*(shorthand)*
implied authority	*(shorthand)*	justifiable cause	*(shorthand)*
inchoate	*(shorthand)*	land contract	*(shorthand)*
incidental authority	*(shorthand)*	leaseholder estates	*(shorthand)*
indemnification	*(shorthand)*	legacy	*(shorthand)*
indigent	*(shorthand)*	legatee	*(shorthand)*
indorsement	*(shorthand)*	letter of credit	*(shorthand)*
inland bill of exchange	*(shorthand)*	liens on realty	*(shorthand)*
installment note	*(shorthand)*	life estate	*(shorthand)*
Instruments of credit	*(shorthand)*	liquidating partners	*(shorthand)*

material alteration	*(shorthand)*	quarters of coverage	*(shorthand)*
monthly tenancy	*(shorthand)*	quitclaim deed	*(shorthand)*
mortality table	*(shorthand)*	quo warranto proceedings	*(shorthand)*
mortgagor	*(shorthand)*	real defenses	*(shorthand)*
municipal corporation	*(shorthand)*	real estate mortgage	*(shorthand)*
National Labor Relations Act	*(shorthand)*	registered bonds	*(shorthand)*
negotiability	*(shorthand)*	release deed	*(shorthand)*
negotiable instruments	*(shorthand)*	restrictive indorsement	*(shorthand)*
no-par-value stock	*(shorthand)*	reversion estate	*(shorthand)*
partner by estoppel	*(shorthand)*	riders	*(shorthand)*
pilferage	*(shorthand)*	right of contribution	*(shorthand)*
postdated	*(shorthand)*	right of indemnification	*(shorthand)*
preferred stock	*(shorthand)*	right of lien	*(shorthand)*
presentment	*(shorthand)*	right of subrogation	*(shorthand)*
presumption of consideration	*(shorthand)*	satisfaction piece	*(shorthand)*
probate court	*(shorthand)*	scope of authority	*(shorthand)*
promissory notes	*(shorthand)*	Social Security Act	*(shorthand)*
property damage insurance	*(shorthand)*	standard short-rate scale	*(shorthand)*
prorata clauses	*(shorthand)*	statute of frauds	*(shorthand)*
public liability insurance	*(shorthand)*		

stock company	*Sk co*
straight life policy	*Sa li plc*
supplementary benefits	*spl ry bnfl*
suretyship	*zury zp*
tenancy at will	*lnc l l*
tenancy in common	*lnc n kmn*
title by prescription	*lil b pskpy*
title insurance	*lil nzuy*
Torrens system	*lns SSm*
ultra vires acts	*ula vry ak*
undisclosed principal	*udky prpl*
vacancy clause	*vknc kz*
valued policy	*vlu plc*
waiver of notice	*wvr v nls*
waiver indorsement	*wvr nds*
way of necessity	*wa v nss*
watered stock	*wlr Sk*
workmens compensation law	*WCL*
writ of mandamus	*rl m ms*

abdominal	*abdmnl*	cardiographic	*k gfk*
absorbent gland	*absb g*	cardioneurosis	*k nrss*
acid cell	*asd sl*	cardiovascular	*k vsklr*
acromegaly	*akmgl*	carminative	*knmv*
adenalgia	*anlja*	carotid gland	*ktd g*
adenoidectomy	*anydkme*	cataract	*klrk*
adipose duct	*adpz dk*	catgut	*klgl*
aorta	*a la*	celialgia	*sllga*
appendectomy	*ap kme*	celiotomy	*sllme*
arterial gland	*rtl g*	celiorrhaphy	*slrfe*
autopsy	*alpse*	cephalic vein	*sfla va*
bacteriological	*bklrljkl*	cerebellum	*srblm*
benign tumor	*bne tmr*	cerebral	*srbl*
bicarbonate of soda	*bkbnl v sda*	cholera	*klra*
bichloride of mercury	*bkry v mky*	cirrhosis	*srss*
blood count	*bd k*	clonic spasm	*knk spzm*
blood gland	*bd g*	contusion	*kly*
blood vessels	*bd vsl*	compound fracture	*kp fcu*
bone cell	*bo sl*	concussion of the brain	*bky v ba*
bronchial	*bgl*	conglomerate gland	*kgmra g*
calcification	*ksfkj*	corneal	*knl*
carcinoma	*ksnma*	corneal cell	*knl sl*
cardiac glands	*k k g*	corpuscular	*kpsklr*

183

cylindric cell	*sl k sl*	fiber cell	*fbr sl*
cystic tumor	*sSk tmr*	filiform	*flfm*
debility	*dbly*	formaldehyde	*fmdhi*
dementia precox	*dmya pky*	frontal veins	*fl va*
dentin cell	*d n sl*	ganglion	*gagln*
dermatosis	*dmlss*	gangrene	*gare*
dermoid tumor	*dmyd tmr*	gastralgia	*gsly*
desmoid tumor	*dsmyd tmr*	gastrostomy	*gstme*
dicrotic	*dklk*	genupecteral	*gnpkrl*
dilatation	*dlly*	gnathic	*n k*
dyspnea	*dpna*	gutteral duct	*gtl dk*
elephantiasis	*lf ss*	hemorrhage	*hmry*
emissary vein	*may va*	hypodermic injection	*hpdmk hyky*
endocarditis	*ndk ls*	ichthyosis	*ik ss*
engorgement	*ngj*	infraclavicular	*nfkuklr*
enzyme	*nyu*	inoperable	*nopb*
epidermic cells	*epdmk sl*	insufflation	*nsfly*
epidermis	*epdms*	insulin	*nsln*
epiglottis	*epgls*	inter-cricothyrotomy	*nkik rtme*
eructation	*erkly*	intermittent fever	*nml fvr*
erysipelas	*erspls*	inunction of mercury	*nyk v mky*
esophagus	*esfgs*	iridectomy	*irdkme*
eustachian	*usy*	iridotomy	*irdtme*
false tumor	*fs tmr*		

184

ischemia	*(shorthand)*	morphology	*(shorthand)*
jugular vein	*(shorthand)*	myalgia	*(shorthand)*
knee-chest	*(shorthand)*	myasthenia	*(shorthand)*
lacrimal duct	*(shorthand)*	myoma	*(shorthand)*
laparectomy	*(shorthand)*	myorrhaphy	*(shorthand)*
laparotomy	*(shorthand)*	myotomy	*(shorthand)*
laudanum	*(shorthand)*	nasal duct	*(shorthand)*
lithotome	*(shorthand)*	nasopharyngeal	*(shorthand)*
locomotor ataxia	*(shorthand)*	nephralgia	*(shorthand)*
macrocephalic	*(shorthand)*	nephrostomy	*(shorthand)*
macrocornea	*(shorthand)*	nephrotomy	*(shorthand)*
macrocyst	*(shorthand)*	neuralgia	*(shorthand)*
macrognathia	*(shorthand)*	node	*(shorthand)*
macrophage	*(shorthand)*	nodule	*(shorthand)*
macrosis	*(shorthand)*	nosology	*(shorthand)*
mandible	*(shorthand)*	nux vomica	*(shorthand)*
median vein	*(shorthand)*	olfactory cells	*(shorthand)*
medulla oblongata	*(shorthand)*	ophthalmia	*(shorthand)*
meso-appendix	*(shorthand)*	ophthalmiatrics	*(shorthand)*
microcephalus	*(shorthand)*	orthopedic	*(shorthand)*
miliary gland	*(shorthand)*	ostalgia	*(shorthand)*
mitral stenosis	*(shorthand)*	ostectomy	*(shorthand)*
moribound condition	*(shorthand)*	otalgia	*(shorthand)*
		otectomy	*(shorthand)*
		otiatrics	*(shorthand)*

palatal	*pll*	rigor mortis	*rgr m s*
paminiform	*pnmfm*	salivation	*slvy*
pancreatic	*pnklk*	scar tissue	*skr tzu*
paranoia	*pnya*	sclerotomy	*slrlme*
paratyphoid	*plfyd*	serous	*sr*
parotid	*ptd*	serpiginous	*sppnu*
patellar reflex	*ptlr rfx*	small pox	*sml px*
pediatrics	*pdlk*	spastic	*spSk*
pemphigoid	*pmfgyd*	splenalgia	*spnly*
phlebalgia	*fly*	specialist	*spuS*
phlebectomy	*fbkme*	splenic tumor	*spnk tmr*
phleborraphy	*fbrfe*	splenic vein	*spnk va*
phlebotomy	*fblme*	splenorraphy	*spnfe*
pituitary	*plly*	strabismus	*Sbzms*
pleural cavity	*plrl kus*	suppuration	*spy*
pneumococcus	*nmkks*	superficially	*sprfxl*
polypnea	*plpna*	tarsectomy	*lskme*
post mortem	*psm m*	taste cells	*tS sl*
probang	*pbg*	tegmental cells	*tgm l sl*
pruritus	*prls*	thoracalgia	*rkly*
pustule	*psu*	thoracostomy	*rkSme*
pyloric glands	*plrkg*	tonsillectomy	*tnslkme*
pyonephritis	*pnfrls*	tonsillotomy	*tnsllme*
radial vein	*rdl va*	trachealgia	*tkly*
red blood cells	*rd bd sl*	tracheostomy	*tkSme*

186

transition tumor	*[shorthand]*
turgescence	*[shorthand]*
ulnar vein	*[shorthand]*
vaso-motor	*[shorthand]*
venomotor	*[shorthand]*
volar	*[shorthand]*
white blood cells	*[shorthand]*
white blood corpuscles	*[shorthand]*

accelerated	*xlra*	conducted	*kdk*
acceleration	*xlry*	cone	*ko*
accumulators	*agmlar*	configuration	*kfgry*
aerodynamics	*ardmnk*	control/s	*Kl*
analytical	*anllkl*	coolant	*kl*
attitude	*allu*	criteria	*klra*
alternator	*alnar*	contractual	*Kkx*
assembly	*asml*	controllability	*KlB,*
atsmospheric	*almsfrk*	defensive	*dfrv*
authorization	*a rzy*	descent	*ds*
axis	*ays*	descend/s	*ds*
booster	*bSr*	density	*dnsy*
budget	*byl*	design	*dzy*
calculators	*lkllr*	development	*dvlp*
calibrate	*klba*	diagonal	*dgnl*
camber	*kmbr*	drag	*dg*
certified	*st*	droppable	*dpB*
centrifugal force	*s fgl fs*	engine	*nyn*
chamber	*cmbr*	extensive	*xly,*
chute	*zu*	fabrication	*fbkj*
communication	*kmnkj*	fin	*fn*
compatibility	*kplB,*	finalize	*fnly*
comparable	*kpB*	fire	*fr*
components	*kpn*	formalize	*fmly*
comprehensive	*kpsv*	fuel	*fu*

functional		pertinent	
guidance		pitot tube	
generator		pitch	
hydraulic		plastic	
increment		pressure	
inflammable		potential	
injector		practicable	
impulse		proficiency	
integrated		propellant	
intensive		propulsion	
internal		prototype	
jet		radar	
launch		radius	
lateral		ratio	
liaison		reactive	
longitudinal		reconnaissance	
magnesium		regenerative	
mandatory		regulation	
maneuverability		reliability	
motor		replaceable	
nose cone		roll	
operable		rotated	
oxidizer		segregate	
payload		sequence	
performance		slot	

span	*spn*	velocity	*vlsy*
spin	*spn*	vehicle	*vhkl*
stability	*SBy*	visibility	*vzby*
static	*Slk*	volume	*vlm*
structure	*Sku*	yaw	*ya*
strut	*Sl*		
subsidies	*ssde*		
supremacy	*spmc*		
tapering	*tprg*		
target/s	*tgt*		
technical	*tknkl*		
technique	*tkne*		
telemetry	*tlmly*		
telemetering	*tlmlrg*		
temperature	*tmpcu*		
termination	*tmny*		
test	*t8*		
testing	*t8g*		
theoretical	*rtkl*		
thermal	*ml*		
thrust	*r8*		
tolerance	*tly*		
trajectory	*tjkly*		
transportable	*tp8*		
unstable	*uSB*		